Manual of Intelligence Operations

Attention Authors

Manas Publications is fighting a war to tell the world that India can win the battle not only by the bullet but also by pen. We are converting fighters into writers. There is no dearth of intellectuals in our country, however, their knowledge is confined to them only. No sincere effort has been made by any other publisher to channelise their knowledge, which is why the talent of every intellectual remains latent. An author always presents the raw material in the shape of a manuscript and it is the job of the publisher to convert it to a finished product. Manas has been continually motivating intellectuals and publishing their manuscripts for more than two decades and would like to publish your manuscript too. If you or your colleagues have a manuscript ready for publication or are working on it, contact us with a detailed synopsis and list of contents. Manas will also suggest you a suitable title for writing related to your area of expertise. Manas is known for its publishing quality. We take utmost care in publishing and also give wide publicity to the book and its author through our national and international distribution network.

Manual of Intelligence Operations

US Marine Corps

Manas Publications
(We Convert Fighters into Writers)
New Delhi-110002 (INDIA)

MANAS PUBLICATIONS
(Publishers, Distributors, Importers & Exporters)
4402/5-A, Ansari Road
(Opp. HDFC Bank)
Darya Ganj, New Delhi-110 002 (INDIA)
Off. © 23260783, 23265523, Res. © 23842660
Fax: 011-23272766
E-mail: manaspublications@vsnl.com
manaspublications@gmail.com
www.manaspublications.in

ISBN 978-81-7049-388-4
Rs. 595

Typeset at
Manas Publications

Printed in India at
RK Print Services, Delhi
and published by Mrs Suman Lata for
Manas Publications, 4402/5-A, Ansari Road
(Opp. HDFC Bank),
Darya Ganj, New Delhi-110 002 (INDIA)

Contents

Chapter - 1

Fundamentals

Intelligence is knowledge of the battlespace and of the threat forces in that battlespace. Knowledge is generated in support of the commander's decision making process and is the result of the collection, processing, exploitation, evaluation, integration, analysis, and interpretation of available information about the battlespace and threat.

INTELLIGENCE OBJECTIVES

Intelligence has two objectives: to reduce uncertainty by providing accurate, timely, and relevant knowledge about the threat and the surrounding environment, and to assist in protecting friendly forces (to include Department of Defence [DOD] personnel, family members, resources, facilities and critical information) through counterintelligence (CI).

Uncertainty pervades the battlespace—it is a fundamental attribute of war. First and foremost, intelligence should support the commander's decisionmaking process by reducing uncertainty about the hostile situation. Intelligence should accomplish the following actions to achieve this objective:

- Identify and evaluate existing conditions and capabilities.
- On the basis of those existing conditions and capabilities, estimate possible enemy courses of action (COAs) and provide insight into possible future actions.
- Aid in identifying friendly critical vulnerabilities that the threat may exploit.
- Assist in developing and evaluating friendly COAs.

The fog and friction of war will never allow the commander to have a perfect picture of the battlespace. Because intelligence deals with the greatest number of unknowns—questions about an unfamiliar area and a hostile enemy who is actively trying to conceal information about his forces and intentions—there will almost always be gaps in intelligence, and the knowledge provided will lack the desired degree of detail and reliability. Intelligence cannot provide absolute certainty. It attempts to reduce the uncertainty facing the commander to a reasonable level by collecting relevant information, placing it in context to provide knowledge, and conveying it in the form of images to enhance understanding.

CI is information gathered and activities conducted to protect against espionage, other intelligence activities, sabotage or assassinations conducted by or on behalf of foreign governments or elements thereof, foreign organizations, foreign persons or international terrorist activities.

CI activities consist of active and passive measures, functions, and services. CI measures, functions, and services are intended to deny a potential adversary information that might increase the effectiveness of hostile operations against friendly forces; detect and neutralize foreign intelligence collection; and deceive the enemy as to friendly capabilities and intentions. In so doing, CI increases uncertainty for the enemy, thereby making a significant contribution to the success of operations. CI services identify friendly vulnerabilities, evaluate security measures, and assist in implementing appropriate plans to enhance a unit's force protection posture against the threats of sabotage, subversion, and terrorism.

MANOEUVRE WARFARE

The essence of war is a violent clash between independent wills, each trying to impose itself on the other. War's defining attributes of friction, uncertainty, fluidity, disorder, and complexity combine with the various dimensions of human nature to make war a fundamentally unpredictable activity. To succeed in war, Marines must be able to operate effectively in this uncertain, chaotic, complex, and fluid environment.

The Marine Corps philosophy for winning under these conditions is based on rapid, flexible, and opportune manoeuvre. MCDP 1, *Warfighting*, states that, "Manoeuvre warfare is a warfighting philosophy that seeks to shatter the enemy's cohesion through a variety of rapid, focused, and unexpected actions which create a turbulent and rapidly deteriorating situation with which the enemy cannot cope." Manoeuvre warfare requires manoeuvre in time and space to achieve superiority over the enemy. It concentrates on those actions that present the enemy with a series of dilemmas where events happen unexpectedly and faster than the enemy can react. Concepts central to executing manoeuvre warfare follow:

Orienting on the enemy: Manoeuvre warfare attacks the enemy "system," the combination of physical, moral, and mental components that make up an enemy or an enemy force. This means focusing outward on the particular characteristics of the enemy.

Centers of gravity (COG) and critical vulnerabilities: COG are sources of moral or physical strength, power or resistance that are critical to the enemy's ability to resist. Critical vulnerabilities are components of the enemy system that are both crucial to the functioning of the system and vulnerable to exploitation. Identifying and exploiting an enemy's COG and critical vulnerabilities help focus combat power toward a decisive aim.

Main effort: The main effort is the unit assigned responsibility to accomplish the key mission within the command. It is directed where there is the best opportunity to succeed and at the objective that will have the most significant effect on the enemy, normally a critical vulnerability.

Commander's intent: Commander's intent describes the purpose behind the task assigned in a mission. It provides continuing guidance when the tactical situation changes and permits the exercise of initiative in harmony with the commander's desires.

Mission tactics: Mission tactics assign subordinates a task without specifying how it must be accomplished. They permit subordinates to exercise initiative in adapting to ever-changing situations.

Tempo: Tempo keeps the enemy off balance, thereby increasing his friction. Speed, initiative, and flexibility generate and maintain a tempo that the enemy cannot match.

Accurate and timely intelligence is a prerequisite for success in manoeuvre warfare. Manoeuvre warfare is based on a firm focus on the enemy and on taking action that avoids enemy strengths and exploits enemy critical vulnerabilities. It means acting in a manner and at a time and place that the enemy does not expect and is not prepared. It requires decision and action based on situational awareness—a keen understanding of the factors that make each situation unique. Intelligence provides the knowledge of the enemy and the battlespace that permits the commander to reduce uncertainty, identify opportunities for success. assess risk, outline intent, and make decisions that provide focus, generate speed and tempo, and achieve decisive results.

DEVELOPING INTELLIGENCE

Data, Information, and Intelligence

Intelligence is not simply another term for information. Intelligence is more than an element of Intelligence Operations data or a grouping of information; it is a body of knowledge. Knowledge occupies a unique place in the information hierarchy, which is a framework to distinguish between various classes of information. (See figure 1-1.)

There is a clear and important distinction between raw data, information, and intelligence. Intelligence is not a mass of unfocused data or even a collection of related facts. In fact, giving a commander every piece of data without providing meaning can increase uncertainty by overloading the commander with incomplete. contradictory or irrelevant information. To be intelligence, data must be placed in context to provide an accurate and meaningful image of the hostile situation. Intelligence is developed by analyzing and synthesizing data and information to produce knowledge about the threat and the environment. The

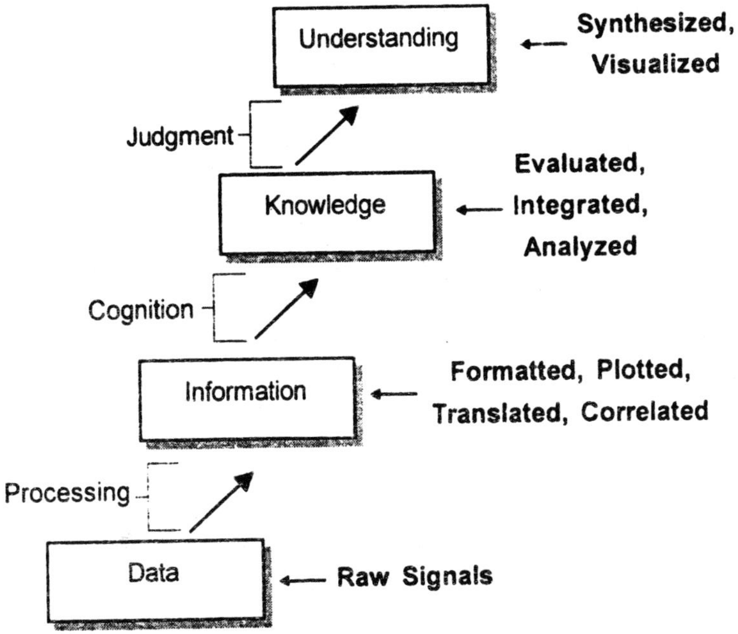

Figure 1-1. *The Information Hierarchy.*

commander combines this knowledge with knowledge of the friendly situation and employs experience, judgment, and intuition to understand the situation. The commander then applies this understanding in making decisions.

The Intelligence Cycle

Intelligence is the output of a process that converts data and information into knowledge that applies to a specific military decision. The process used to develop intelligence is called the intelligence cycle. This cycle is the process by which information is planned for. obtained. assembled. converted through analysis into intelligence, provided to decisionmakers. and, ultimately, used in making decisions. (See figure 1-2.)

The intelligence cycle consists of a series of related activities that translate the need for intelligence about a particular aspect of the battlespace or threat into a knowledge-based product that is provided to the commander for use in the decisionmaking

Intelligence Cycle	Key Considerations
Planning and direction.	Identify intelligence requirements. Plan intelligence operations and activities. Support the formulation of the commander's estimate of the situation.
Collection.	Develop the required intelligence structure. Use organic, attached, and supporting intelligence sources to collect intelligence.
Processing, exploitation, and production.	Conversion of raw data and information into a suitable form of intelligence.
Dissemination.	Timely provision of intelligence. in appropriate form, to those who need it.
Utilization.	Use of intelligence.

Figure 1-2. *Key Considerations of the Intelligence Cycle.*

process. In this sequence, intelligence needs are identified and a plan is developed for satisfying those needs. Data are collected, processed into information, and converted into intelligence through analysis and synthesis. The resulting knowledge is then provided to the commander as an intelligence product that is used in making decisions. The information used to produce intelligence is derived from a variety of sources. Intelligence information; i.e., information used to generate intelligence, is commonly drawn from three types of data: intelligence, sensor or combat.

Intelligence data are derived from assets primarily dedicated to intelligence collection; e.g., imagery systems, electronic intercept equipment or human intelligence (HUMINT) sources.

Sensor data are derived from sensors whose primary mission is surveillance or target acquisition; e.g., air surveillance radars, counterbattery radars, and remote ground sensors.

Combat data are derived from reporting by operational units. Because of their highly perishable or critical nature, combat data and sensor data are sometimes used to effect decisions without being converted into intelligence. Although the demands of the ongoing battle may require rapid action, decisions based on raw, unprocessed data or single pieces of data should be avoided.

Processing, analysis, and synthesis of data and information into intelligence can be accomplished rapidly at all levels. We seek knowledge—*accurate intelligence*, not incomplete, unfocused, or *unevaluated information*—to enhance our understanding and base our decisions. The intelligence cycle works continuously to satisfy intelligence shortfalls and confirm or refute fragmentary information. Once collected and processed, information is converted into intelligence through the application of experience and judgment. Information is analyzed to determine its significance and is synthesized with other relevant information to build a coherent picture of existing conditions and capabilities. This picture is then used to predict possible outcomes of environmental conditions and enemy actions. Results are conveyed to the commander in an intelligence product. Because humans understand situations best as images—mental pictures—intelligence is produced and disseminated in graphic form whenever possible. The process is completed when the knowledge provided is applied to influence decisionmaking.

INTELLIGENCE OPERATIONS

Intelligence personnel and organizations perform a number of separate and distinct activities and functions that are collectively known as intelligence operations. Intelligence operations are conducted to provide intelligence in support of the decisionmaking process of commanders down to the small-unit level. The primary focus of Marine Corps intelligence operations is generating *tactical intelligence*; i.e., intelligence that supports the planning and conduct of tactical actions. Although the focus is on tactical intelligence, the Marine Corps must draw on both strategic and operational intelligence resources and, in certain circumstances, be prepared to conduct intelligence operations at the operational and even strategic level. Intelligence reduces uncertainty and supports the decisionmaking process by—

- Describing the battlespace.
- Identifying key factors in the battlespace that can influence operations.
- Defining and evaluating threat capabilities.
- Identifying the enemy's COG and critical vulnerabilities.
- Assessing enemy intentions.

Relationship to Command and Control

Intelligence is a fundamental component of command and control (C2). It is the means by which a commander recognizes what needs to be done and sees to it that appropriate actions are taken. A principal aim of C2 is to enhance the commander's ability to make sound and timely decisions. Intelligence facilitates the commander's decisionmaking process by making a major contribution to the understanding of the battlespace and the threat. Intelligence is also an integral element of the process through which the commander implements decisions. Inadequate or imperfect intelligence can significantly inhibit the ability of a commander or subordinates to carry out these decisions. Lack of a continuous, effective intelligence effort also degrades the quality of feedback to the commander about the unfolding situation: it is this feedback that allows the commander to modify the actions of the command as needed.

Because intelligence is crucial to success on the battlefield, it must be given command attention. The commander drives intelligence by focusing the intelligence effort through the definition of the mission, articulation of his intent, and designating priority intelligence requirements (PIRs). A PIR is an intelligence requirement (IR) associated with a decision that will critically affect the overall success of the command's mission. PIRs are a subset of commander's critical information requirements (CCIRs) and are focused on the environment and the threat.

Relationship to Operations

Intelligence is inseparable from operations. Intelligence drives operations by shaping the planning and execution of operations. It provides a menu of factors that the commander considers when making a decision. Specifically, intelligence—

- Identifies potential advantages offered by the environment.
- Describes limitations imposed by the environment.
- Ascertains and assesses enemy strengths to be avoided.
- Uncovers enemy critical vulnerabilities that can be exploited.
- Recommends COAs based on factors of the battlespace and threat.
- Enables rapid decisionmaking and generating and maintaining tempo.

Operational actions develop logically from intelligence. A commander with effective intelligence knows the nature of the terrain, weather conditions, the composition and status of the infrastructure in the area of operations, the makeup and attitude of the population that will be encountered, and how the combined effects of these factors will influence mission accomplishment. Intelligence provides knowledge of threat capabilities, strengths, COG and critical vulnerabilities, along with insight into the enemy's intentions. Integrating intelligence on the threat and the battlespace helps provide the commander with situational awareness, which is used to determine the decisive time and place to strike.

Intelligence and operations must be linked throughout the planning, decision, execution, and assessment (PDE&A) cycle at all levels. Intelligence shapes the plan and provides the knowledge that facilitates execution. It identifies changes in the situation that require modification of the plan or that trigger decisions during the conduct of the operation. At the same time, the nature of the mission and the concept of operations focus and shape the intelligence effort; intelligence that is not relevant to the mission is useless. IRs and intelligence operations are continually evaluated to ensure that they are focused on supporting mission accomplishment.

PRINCIPLES OF INTELLIGENCE OPERATIONS

The focus is on tactical intelligence: The focus of Marine Corps intelligence operations is on the generation of tactical intelligence. However, there are no sharp boundaries between levels of intelligence; they merge and form a continuum. In some instances Marine Corps tactical intelligence operations will support operational and strategic IRs.

Intelligence is focused downward: Intelligence must be available to commanders at all levels. Although the management of intelligence collection and production is centralized in the MAGTF command element (CE), the focus is on providing the intelligence needed to plan and execute the mission to every unit involved in the operation. Requirements of the entire force will be considered in directing the intelligence effort. Critical products will be *pushed* down to the tactical commander, who will be able to *pull* additional intelligence support as needed.

Intelligence drives operations: The Marine Corps' warfighting philosophy depends on timely, accurate intelligence for success. Intelligence is the critical underpinning for each phase of the PDE&A cycle.

Intelligence activities require centralized management: Good intelligence is the result of the integration of many separate and specialized collection, processing, and analytical resources. The scarcity of these assets, coupled with the requirement to focus on the commander's PIRs, creates the need for centralized coordination and management. This centralization will be done in the MAGTF CE, under the direction of intelligence officers who are trained and experienced in the management of multidiscipline, all-source intelligence operations. (Allsource intelligence is intelligence that incorporates all available sources of information in the development of the finished intelligence product.) Although centralized coordination and management is required for efficient and effective use of intelligence assets, it is critical for the commander who is exercising centralized control to allocate appropriate resources to ensure that needs of subordinate commands that are crucial to mission accomplishment are properly addressed.

The G-2/S-2 facilitates use of intelligence: The intelligence officer enables effective use of intelligence throughout the command. As the principal disseminator of intelligence, the intelligence officer ensures that the full implications of the intelligence picture are understood. To do this, the intelligence officer must be a *full and continuous* participant in the planning process.

Intelligence must be tailored and timely: Intelligence must be tailored to the requirements of the user, provided in a useful format, and received in time to affect the decisionmaking process. Delivery of the right intelligence—not simply data or information—to the right place at the right time must be the guiding principle of all dissemination efforts.

Utilization is the final step of the intelligence cycle: Intelligence has no inherent value; its value is derived from its support of decisionmaking. The intelligence cycle is not complete until the intelligence that has been developed is used to plan and/or execute operations. (See figure 1.3.)

INTELLIGENCE FUNCTIONS

All six functions are carried out continually during the PDE&A cycle at all levels throughout the force. However, particular functions may be stressed more during one phase of the cycle. Different units may emphasize one or two functions over the others based on individual missions.

Support the Commander's Estimate

Intelligence supports the formulation and subsequent modification of the commander's estimate of the situation by providing as accurate an image of the battlespace and the threat as possible. Intelligence supports initial planning and decisionmaking. One of the principal tools used in this function is intelligence preparation of the battlespace (IPB). IPB is a

Intelligence Functions	Decisionmaking Operational Activities	
Support to commander's estimate.	Plan a mission.	Develop and analyze COAs.
Situation development.	Execute the mission.	Monitor execution. Modify plan as necessary.
Indications and warning.	Orient on contingencies.	Increase readiness. Develop contingency plans.
Support to force protection.	Force protection.	Support operations security (OPSEC). Nuclear, chemical, and biological defense. Support deception plan.
Support to targeting.	Plan fire support.	Attack targets.
Support to combat assessment.	Reorient forces.	Plan future operations. Consolidate, pursue, exploit. Reattack targets.

Figure 1-3. *Relationship Between Intelligence Functions and Operations.*

systematic, continuous process of analyzing the threat and environment in a specific geographic area. IPB helps to provide an appreciation for the characteristics of the area of operations and the enemy capabilities, weaknesses, and COAs. This knowledge affords the commander an understanding of the battlespace and the opportunity to exploit enemy critical vulnerabilities.

Develop the Situation

Situation development provides continuing knowledge of unfolding events to help update the estimate of the situation. It is a dynamic process that assesses the current situation and confirms or denies the adoption of specific COAs by the enemy. It helps refine our understanding of the battlespace and reduces uncertainty and risk. Situation development occurs during execution and provides the basis for adapting plans or exploiting opportunities.

Provide Indications and Warning

Indications and warning (I&W) serve a protective purpose, providing early warning of potential hostile action. They help prevent surprise and reduce risk from enemy actions that run counter to planning assumptions.

Support Force Protection

Force protection is the set of comprehensive security measures, collection activities, and operations that are undertaken to guard the force against the effects of enemy action. Intelligence supports force protection by identifying, locating, and countering foreign intelligence collection, sabotage, subversion, and terrorism capabilities. Support to force protection requires detailed and accurate assessments of threat force capabilities and intentions and facilitates efforts to deny the enemy the opportunity to take offensive action against our forces.

Support Targeting

Intelligence supports targeting by identifying target systems, critical nodes, and high-value and high-payoff targets as well as by providing the intelligence required to most effectively engage these targets

Support Combat Assessment

Combat assessment is the process used to determine the overall effectiveness of military operations and identify requirements for future actions. Intelligence supports the entire combat assessment process and is directly responsible for battle damage assessment (BDA), which is one of the principal components of combat assessment. BDA is the timely and accurate estimate of the damage resulting from the application of military force. BDA estimates physical damage to a particular target, functional damage to that target, and the capability of the entire target system to continue its operations.

THE COMMANDER'S ROLE IN THE INTELLIGENCE PROCESS

Intelligence is an inherent and essential responsibility of *command.* Commanders must come to think of command and intelligence as inseparable, just as they commonly think of command and operations as inseparable. They must study and understand the theory and the practice of intelligence doctrine. They must be personally involved in the conduct of intelligence activities, and provide guidance, supervision, judgment, and authority to ensure a timely and useful product.

Focus the Intelligence Effort

The commander must provide the guidance and direction necessary for the effective conduct of intelligence activities. Intelligence assets will rarely be sufficient to satisfy every requirement. Thus, the intelligence effort must be focused on clearly articulated priorities that drive the concept of intelligence support and the collection, production, and dissemination efforts. The commander provides this focus through articulating the commander's intent, planning guidance, and the command's PIRs.

Participate in the Intelligence Process

Although the intelligence officer manages the intelligence effort for the commander, the commander is responsible for the results. Effective participation requires an understanding of the practical capabilities and limitations of intelligence personnel, equipment, procedures, and products. The commander should supervise the process, interjecting guidance and direction at key points to ensure that the process is responding to the commander's intent; e.g., the commander should define the scope of the IPB effort, identify the preferred intelligence product format, and establish priorities among subordinate commands' IRs.

Use Intelligence in Decisionmaking

Intelligence exists for the primary purpose of aiding the commander's decisionmaking process. Although the intelligence officer facilitates the use of intelligence throughout the command by providing timely dissemination of the intelligence product and ensuring that the meaning of the intelligence is understood, the commander makes the judgment of its operational impact. The commander makes a personal analysis of the intelligence product and arrives at the estimate of the situation that serves as the basis for the decision. This act is the responsibility of the commander and no one else.

Support the Intelligence Effort

Intelligence is a team effort. Good intelligence is the result of integrating many separate and specialized collection, processing, and analytical resources. Some of these resources are organic to the unit; many are provided by units or agencies outside the command. Intelligence operations by organic assets normally cannot succeed without support from throughout the command. Reconnaissance teams must be inserted, sensors implanted, and communications assets provided for dissemination. Timely and effective intelligence dissemination requires dedicating significant C2 assets. Once an operation begins, nearly every Marine will have the occasion to observe significant facts about the enemy and environment. All personnel should understand and carry out their responsibility to collect and report information. The commander must ensure that all members of the unit understand the importance placed on intelligence and the requirement to support the intelligence effort. External support must be requested and coordinated. The intelligence staff executes the procedures to obtain the required support, but does so in the name of the commander. When the command's support requirements go unsatisfied, the commander must intervene, lending command authority to obtain the support.

Evaluate the Results of Intelligence Activities

The commander must provide feedback to the intelligence support system. Feedback should identify where the intelligence provided met expectations and where and how it fell short. Key areas to evaluate include product content, presentation, timeliness, and overall usefulness. Meaningful evaluation of the intelligence effort provides the basis for its continual improvement.

INFORMATION OPERATIONS

Intelligence support is required to conduct *information operations (IO).* Specific intelligence is required for planning and deconfliction and for employing military disciplines available to achieve IO effects. Intelligence is inextricably linked to facilitating core and supporting IO disciplines in offensive or defensive postures. As a product, intelligence supports IO in the same manner provided to all operations. Planning for IO cannot be conducted without intelligence on adversary information and information systems, perceptions, and critical vulnerabilities in their C2 process. Each capability used in an IO context will have separate and continuous intelligence support requirements. The psychological profiles of adversary commanders and forces are themselves an important element within the overall assessment process.

Planning

Intelligence support to IO planning is conducted as part of the IPB process. One of the key outputs from IPB is an analysis of the desired objectives and/or end states of stakeholders. These desires are usually categorized relative to broad capability. The categories may be elements of national power such as politics, economics, military, and society. Capability analysis processes within IPB also provide detail on stakeholder capacity and intent to conduct or sustain defensive and offensive IO. Intelligence support will aim to define critical nodes and vulnerabilities within the adversary's information structure; these include the key personnel, equipment, procedures and protocols involved in the transfer of information required for successful C2. Such intelligence support will orient key aspects of the operation plan towards the systematic disruption of critical nodes and information bearers. Friendly force staff advice, linked to intelligence advice on adversary COAs and CI advice on the threats to security, provide the operations planning process with the background to decide the protective measures required for own nodes and information bearers. Accurate, timely, and directed intelligence provides the foundation that IO decisions are based.

Intelligence Preparation of the Battlespace

IPB is a continuous process used to develop a detailed knowledge of the adversary's use of information and information systems. Intelligence support for IO planning builds upon traditional IPB and provides the essential basis for planning IO through the following considerations:

- The adversary commander's freedom of action and the freedom of action allowed to subordinates (decisionmaking process). This includes adversary perceptions of the situation (political, social, and cultural influences) and developments.
- Adversary IO capability, intent, morale, and vulnerability to offensive IO.
- C2 aspects such as key personnel, target audiences, headquarters, communication nodes, databases or intelligence collection systems. C2 nodes that appear in more than one adversary COA should be highlighted for targeting.
- Technical knowledge of a wide array of information, C2, intelligence, and media systems.
- Assessments of friendly vulnerability to adversary IO.

IO-Related Force Protection

Knowledge of the threat—adversaries, their intent, and capabilities—is a key consideration in the risk management process. CI and counter-reconnaissance contribute directly to force protection by denying critical information to potential adversaries. Many IO IRs require significant lead-time to develop collection sources, access, and databases. Potential intelligence collection sources should be developed as early as possible; a clear statement of MAGTF IRs is essential. IO will require development of extensive intelligence analytical products to obtain a detailed knowledge of cultural factors, and adversary use of information and information systems.

The Role of Intelligence in IO is Continual

Changes in attitudes, actions, operating patterns, and enemy information systems must be detected, analyzed, and reported to ensure that IO continues to achieve the desired operational effect. Assessing ongoing IO activities is a crucial and extremely challenging responsibility of intelligence as targets must be monitored to determine the effectiveness of the IO efforts. To achieve complete synthesis, IO must be incorporated into the MAGTF's intelligence, BDA, and targeting cycles. The impact of many IO actions may be difficult to measure. Indicators of success or failure must be carefully crafted in advance. Since IO will often not produce the same directly observable effects used for traditional BDA, IO execution will challenge the intelligence system to develop other measures of effectiveness. Once detected, these indicators should be integrated into operational planning and targeting systems, and appropriate action can be taken.

Intelligence enables the planning and execution of successful operations. MAGTF operations are characterized by unity of effort, high tempo, timely decisionmaking, rapid execution, and the relentless exploitation of opportunities. Intelligence operations must have the flexibility, agility, and sustainability to support these types of operations. Expeditionary Manoeuvre Warfare, as the Marine Corps' current capstone concept, lays the foundation for MAGTF operations. MAGTF operations include—

- Operational manoeuvre from the sea (OMFTS).
- Sustained operations ashore.
- Military operations other than war (MOOTW).
- Joint.
- Multinational.

Each operation presents unique challenges and considerations for intelligence support. Many MAGTF operations will be executed as joint operations and with allies, coalition or multinational partners. Intelligence activities in joint and multinational operations require special planning and coordination.

REQUIRED INTELLIGENCE CAPABILITIES

As a warfighting function, intelligence applies broadly across the full range of military operations. The following required intelligence capabilities are common to all operations:

- Conduct intelligence planning and direction.
- Perform intelligence collection management.
- Process and exploit intelligence.
- Produce intelligence.
- Disseminate intelligence.
- Facilitate intelligence's use.
- Perform intelligence, surveillance, reconnaissance, and CI operations.

Chapter - 2

Command and Control

C2 aims to reduce the amount of uncertainty that commanders must accept—to a reasonable point— to make sound decisions. Intelligence is a principal component of C2. Intelligence is a process conducted specifically to aid the commander in decisionmaking by reducing this uncertainty. Intelligence operations support the commander's PDE&A cycle by helping to build situational awareness and providing insight into the nature of the problem facing the commander.

Intelligence provides knowledge concerning the environment and the enemy while furnishing an estimate of potential enemy activities. This knowledge is used by the commander to devise workable, flexible plans; make sound and timely decisions; monitor events to ensure proper execution; and modify decisions quickly in response to changing situations or to exploit fleeting opportunities.

DECISIONMAKING

The principal aim of C2 is to enhance the commander's ability to make sound and timely decisions. Decisionmaking is a time-competitive process that depends in part on the availability of the right elements of information at the right time and place. Without the information that provides the basis of situational awareness, no commander can make sound decisions. Intelligence operations focus on providing the right elements of information concerning the threat and the environment: i.e. intelligence, required to generate situational awareness and fuel the decisionmaking process.

Observe, Orient, Decide, and Act Loop

A simple model that is known as the observe, orient, decide, and act (OODA) loop is used to describe the C2 process. (See figure 2-1.)

The OODA loop applies to any two-sided conflict, whether combatants are individuals or large military formations. When engaged in conflict, participants—

- **Observe.** Take in information about the environment, the friendly status, and the threat.
- **Orient.** Make estimates, assumptions, analyses, and judgments about the situation to create a cohesive mental image.
- **Decide.** Determine what needs to be done, whether it is an immediate reaction or a deliberate plan.
- **Act.** Put the decision into action.

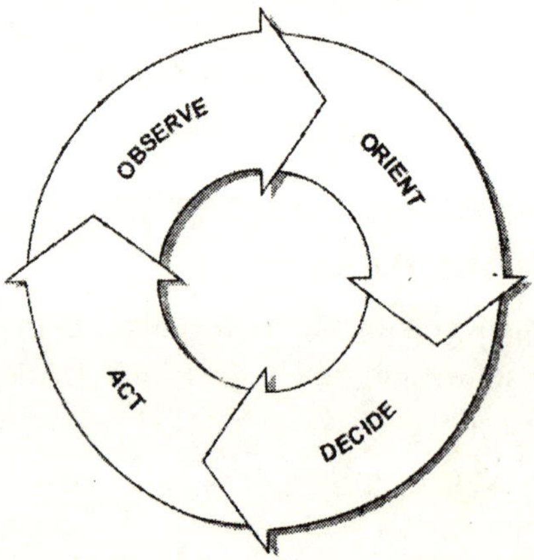

Figure 2-1. *The Observe, Orient, Decide, and Act Loop.*

The OODA loop reflects how decisionmaking is a continual, cyclical process. In any conflict, the participant who can consistently and effectively cycle through the OODA loop faster—

who can maintain a higher tempo of action—gains an increasing advantage with each cycle. The essential lesson of the OODA loop is the importance of generating and maintaining tempo.

Intelligence and the OODA Loop

Intelligence supports all phases of the OODA loop. Intelligence operations facilitate the exercise of C2 by helping to reduce the uncertainty confronting the commander, providing a significant part of the knowledge needed to reach the decision, and assisting in monitoring the implementation and effects of that decision.

Observe: Intelligence collection operations observe threat activity and current environmental conditions. All-source analysis of the collected intelligence information is provided to enhance the commander's situational awareness and understanding of the battlespace.

Orient: The image of the battlespace presented by intelligence, coupled with the predictive analysis of the IPB process, helps orient the commander. It aids in comparing the current situation to the desired end state and in identifying COAs to achieve that end state.

Decide: Intelligence enables decisionmaking by helping define what is operationally possible and most advantageous. It provides the framework for assessing the potential COAs against existing environmental conditions and threat capabilities, vulnerabilities, and likely responses.

Act: Intelligence supports execution by providing a shared picture of the battlespace to all levels of command and by meeting the intelligence needs of all levels of commanders involved in the conduct of operations. Once the concept of operations has been formulated, the focus of intelligence activities shifts from developing the wide-scope intelligence required for COA selection to providing detailed, tailored intelligence to support mission planning and execution. Intelligence is also critical to generating and maintaining tempo in C2. During execution, supporting intelligence operations are conducted to monitor enemy reactions, protect the force from enemy counteraction, and assess the effects of ongoing operations. The continuing intelligence development effort aids the commander in effectively cycling through the OODA loop faster to gain an increasing advantage over the enemy.

Decisionmaking Approaches: Analytical and Intuitive

In analytical decisionmaking, several options for solving the problem at hand are identified, studied, and compared to arrive at the best solution. In intuitive decisionmaking, the commander assesses the situation to recognize a pattern. Once a pattern is identified, experience and judgment guide the commander in evaluating the key elements of the problem and rapidly determining a satisfactory solution. Each approach has different strengths and weaknesses; although conceptually distinct, the two are rarely mutually exclusive.

Intelligence supports analytical decisionmaking by helping to identify the options available and provide the framework (in the form of estimates and studies focused on the threat and key factors of the battlespace) for analysis and comparison of those options. Intelligence supports intuitive decisionmaking by providing the knowledge that helps the commander to recognize emerging patterns. The same methodology is used to develop intelligence support for both decisionmaking approaches. Application of that methodology will vary based on the specifics of each situation and the decisionmaking style of the supported commander. The goal remains the same: to provide a knowledge-based intelligence product that can be applied to make a sound decision.

THE PLANNING, DECISION, EXECUTION, AND ASSESSMENT CYCLE

The PDE&A cycle provides a framework for implementing C2. It translates the cognitive process of the OODA loop into a concrete series of actions taken by the commander and the staff to plan and execute an operation. To be effective, intelligence operations must be linked to the commander's decisionmaking process and the resulting operational activity. Therefore, intelligence operations are integrated with the PDE&A cycle. Specific intelligence tasks are carried out to support each phase of this cycle. While the level of command, time available, and specific tactical situation will influence how the PDE&A cycle is carried out and the degree of detail applied in performing intelligence activities, the same basic intelligence development process is employed in deliberate and rapid planning scenarios and supports analytical and intuitive decisionmaking.

Intelligence support to planning begins with providing a basic description of the environmental conditions and enemy situation in the projected area of operations (AO). As plans are developed and refined, the intelligence effort becomes more narrowly focused on identifying the enemy's critical vulnerabilities and potential COAs and generating mission-specific intelligence products that support detailed planning and execution of specific operational activities. Finally, during mission execution, intelligence operations concentrate on the satisfaction of requirements linked to key operational decisions and the recognition of exploitable opportunities as they arise in the battlespace.

INTELLIGENCE SUPPORT TO PLANNING

Planning is the process of developing practical schemes for taking future actions. It represents an effort to project operational concepts and designs forward in time and space. During the planning process, the commander assesses the situation, builds a vision of the battlespace, and develops the desired outcome of the battle or campaign. Planning is oriented on the future because the primary objective of intelligence is to reduce uncertainty about the future. Intelligence makes a critical contribution to this process. Much of the intelligence effort is "front loaded" to support planning; a substantial portion of intelligence development must be completed during this phase. Intelligence provides a comprehensive image of the battlespace and the threat and helps commanders to provide for constant or predictable aspects of the environment, come to an understanding on the general direction

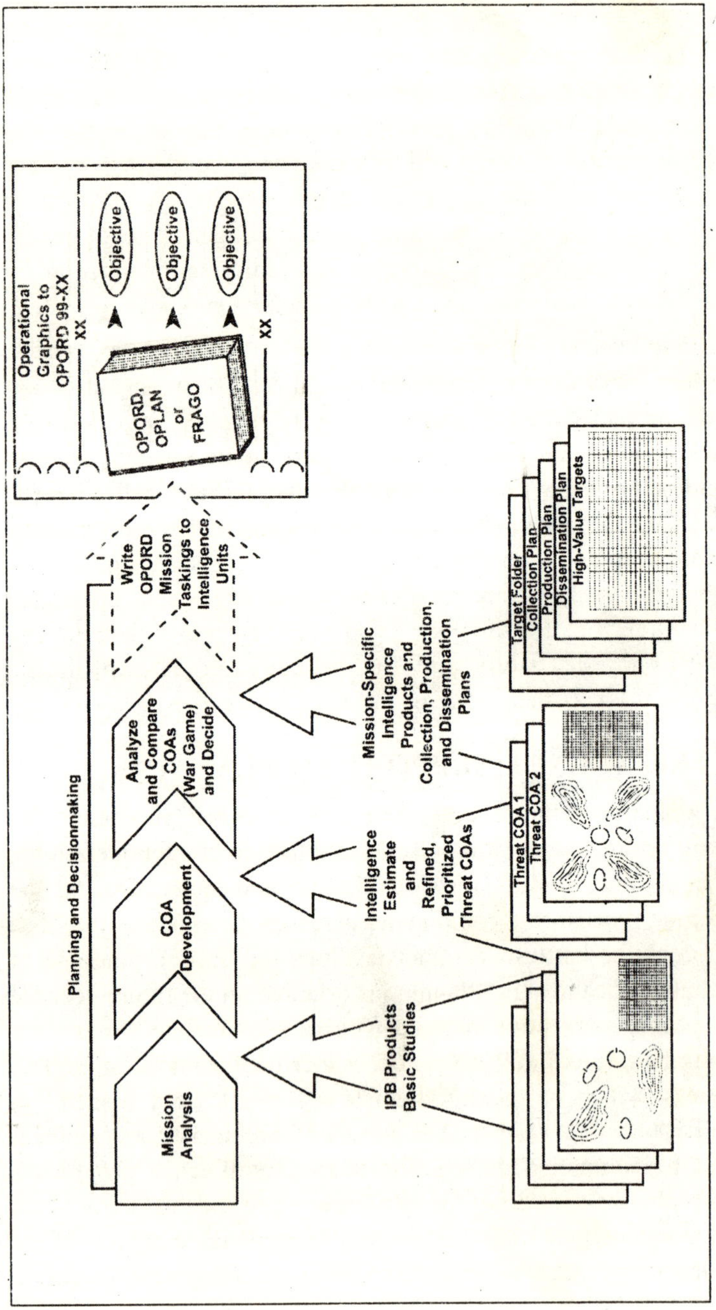

Figure 2-2. *Intelligence Support to Planning.*

of future actions, and anticipate possible threat force actions and reactions.

Planning Models

The choice of planning model is made on the basis of a variety of factors, including the mission, level of command, command relationships, time available, and preferences of individual commanders. All planning models have the same basic elements in common. They—

- Determine what needs to be done.
- Identify one or more COAs to accomplish the required tasks.
- Study the COAs to test feasibility, identify support requirements, and select the most promising alternative.
- Convey instructions to subordinates to execute the plan.

Intelligence development follows the same basic process, no matter which planning model is used. While the specific steps and sequence used in planning may vary, the requirement to provide focused, continuous intelligence to shape the planning process remains constant. A generic planning model will be used to outline the baseline methodology for providing intelligence support to planning. The components of this generic model are mission analysis, COA development, COA analysis, and plan/orders development. For a more complete discussion of planning and the planning process, see MCDP 5, Planning, and MCWP 5-1, *Marine Corps Planning Process.*

Mission Analysis

Mission analysis is conducted to identify the tasks required to accomplish the mission, develop baseline knowledge of the situation, and determine what additional information is required to facilitate the planning process. Intelligence supports mission analysis through providing basic intelligence on the nature of the AO and the threat. Intelligence operations are guided by the results of mission analysis: formulation of initial commander's intent, planning guidance, and PIRs.

Mission Receipt

The receipt of the mission starts the formal planning cycle. However, preliminary planning is normally conducted before the receipt of a mission to anticipate future taskings and potential actions required to accomplish those taskings. Intelligence, in performing its I&W function, will monitor a command's area of interest and identify developing crisis situations and/or potential missions. The commander uses this information to anticipate future missions and to direct the staff to accomplish preliminary planning and intelligence development before the arrival of formal mission tasking. Much of this preliminary work is carried out by the intelligence section, including collecting basic data on the threat and the environment, IPB analysis, and disseminating intelligence throughout the staff.

Information Requirements and Exchange

The process of identifying IRs and gathering and distributing information within the staff, and throughout the command, begins during preliminary planning and intensifies once the mission is received. Intelligence is provided about threat forces and the AO, focusing on the advantages and limitations presented by the environment and the strengths and critical vulnerabilities of the threat. This intelligence is disseminated through a variety of media: the distribution of basic products (maps, imagery, and threat forces studies); the conduct of orientation briefings, and IPB analysis. The continuous, interactive process of IR development also begins. Products provided by the intelligence section stimulate additional questions from the commander and members of the staff. These questions are translated into new or refined IRs. The new requirements are then used to focus the intelligence development process.

Mission Analysis

The commander makes a critical contribution to the operation during this step, setting the stage for the completion of planning and mission execution. During mission analysis, the commander and the staff draw together all available intelligence and information, focus it on the assigned mission, develop an understanding of the tasks to be accomplished, and formulate a rough concept of how to best accomplish those tasks. The result is an initial statement of commander's intent and commander's planning guidance that focuses the remainder of the planning process.

The intelligence officer is a full participant in mission analysis. During mission analysis, the intelligence officer does the following:

- Orients the commander and the other members of the staff to the battlespace and the nature of the threat.
- Aids in forming the commander's intent by helping to define what is operationally possible and most advantageous. This is accomplished primarily through IPB and the analytical process. These results identify the threat's COG, strengths, and critical vulnerabilities and indicate the potential advantages and limitations imposed by the environment.
- Receives guidance from the commander to help shape the intelligence effort. Guidance can take a variety of forms: a statement of commander's intent, a list of PIRs or direct instructions from the commander about intelligence needs or concerns.

COA Development

Building on the knowledge gained through mission analysis, the commander and staff next develop a concept for carrying out the required tasks that embodies the commander's intent and planning guidance. This concept (or COA) encompasses general schemes for the execution of maneuver, fires, logistics, and other supporting functions necessary for successful implementation of the basic concept.

When time permits, the staff usually develops several COAs on the basis of the commander's intent and planning guidance. Intelligence supports this process by the following:

- Continuously updating the view of the battlespace.
- Defining operational possibilities through the IPB process.

- Identifying intelligence gaps that cannot be filled by organic collection assets.
- Providing the focus on the enemy through identifying the threat's COG, critical vulnerabilities, and potential COAs, emphasizing the most likely and most dangerous of these COAs.
- Ensuring that the commander and staff receive, understand, and use relevant, focused, knowledge-based intelligence that enhances their understanding of the situation, rather than a stream of unfocused information.

The intelligence officer interacts with the staff throughout the COA development process, integrating continuing intelligence development efforts with the potential COAs in an effort to ensure that intelligence will be available to support any COA selected.

When an intuitive approach is used, intelligence helps the commander recognize emerging patterns, identify a workable solution, and rapidly evaluate that solution. Products developed through the IPB process present intelligence in the form of images that permit decisionmakers to quickly visualize the situation, see patterns, and assess potential alternatives.

COA War Game

After COAs are developed, they are analyzed and compared to identify the best COA and the concept of operations to implement that COA. Time permitting, the staff conducts a detailed analysis of each COA; each principal staff officer prepares a formal estimate of supportability. When possible, COAs should be wargamed to predict the action, reaction, and counterreaction dynamics of each COA.

Intelligence assists COA analysis by the following:

- Identifying and refining threat COAs and actions/reactions to friendly COAs under consideration.
- Playing the role of the enemy in the wargaming process.
- Developing an independent evaluation of each friendly COA based on an understanding of the environment and

the potential threat response and the ability to provide intelligence support to that COA.

- Helping to focus the staff on the factors of the environment and the enemy, emphasizing the degree of uncertainty and resulting risk associated with each COA.

The intelligence officer's full participation is crucial to successful COA analysis. It is during this step that the full implications of the intelligence estimate are absorbed and applied. To maximize this contribution, the intelligence officer must be able to "think red"—analyze the situation from the enemy's perspective—and "think blue"—understand the intent and construct of friendly plans and operations. Combining these two perspectives enables the intelligence officer to assess the potential effects of threat force actions on the potential COAs.

When time is not available to wargame and conduct a complete COA analysis, the commander makes a rapid mental assessment of available options. The situational awareness that is provided in large part through intelligence guides the commander in evaluating these options and quickly selecting one that offers potential for success.

ORDERS DEVELOPMENT

Based on the COA analysis, the commander selects a COA, refines the intent, and gives further guidance on developing the detailed concept of operations and supporting plans or orders. The emphasis of the intelligence effort, which is focused on the commander's intent, the selected COA, and the identified PIRs, shifts from developing basic and broad-scope intelligence in support of conceptual planning to providing specific intelligence that facilitates functional planning, detailed planning, and mission execution. The intelligence tasks of I&W and supporting the commander's estimate continue, but situation development, support to targeting, and support to force protection now receive increased emphasis.

A concept of intelligence support is prepared to allocate intelligence resources in accordance with the main effort and the concept of operations. COA analysis and wargaming results are used to develop and implement collection, production, and dissemination plans to support the chosen COA. IPB efforts are intensified in an effort to satisfy PIRs and develop the in-depth intelligence required for the detailed planning of specific operational activities. Intelligence sections prepare and disseminate products that embody the results of the IPB process and intelligence collection activities to provide a shared view of the battlespace at all levels of the force. At the same time, they deliver mission-specific intelligence in response to the extensive and precise functional and detailed planning requirements of units that will execute the operation. CI plans and measures are prepared and implemented to conceal our intentions and protect the force. Results of these intelligence activities shape and develop the overall plan/order and the plan's comprehensive supporting annexes and appendices.

EXECUTION

During execution, the plan is refined, implemented, and adapted in response to changes in the situation and action/reaction of the enemy. C2 is a process that generates swift, appropriate, and decisive action and provides a means of continuously assessing developments that provide the basis for adapting. The commander uses a variety of techniques and measures to supervise, monitor, and modify the execution of the plan, thereby shaping the battle and maintaining unity of effort. The intelligence effort must be responsive to the needs of mission execution and ensure a continuous flow of intelligence throughout the force to maintain a shared picture of the battlespace and satisfy new requirements developed by the operating forces.

Intelligence operations are integrated with the concept of operations to enhance force protection, develop situational awareness, and support combat assessment. The results of these operations are used to modify the plan or exercise tactical options, thereby enabling rapid decisionmaking as well as generating and maintaining tempo. The information developed through these activities is entered into the continuous intelligence development process, which provides the basis for planning future operations.

Intelligence support to execution differs in significant ways from intelligence support to planning. First, while intelligence support to planning requires developing a large volume of basic intelligence and preparing broad-scope estimates to develop and analyze COAs, intelligence support to execution involves the satisfaction of a much larger body of IRs in a significantly greater degree of detail. For example, during COA development, it may be sufficient to tell a MAGTF or ground combat element (GCE) commander that an enemy mechanized force is located in a general area and has an approximate number of tanks and armored personnel carriers of various types. However, the subordinate unit tasked with establishing a blocking position opposite that enemy force will require more detailed information on enemy disposition. In another example, the nature of the intelligence required by a Marine Expeditionary Unit (MEU) commander to decide if a raid or tactical recovery of aircraft and personnel (TRAP) mission is feasible is fundamentally different from the type and detail of intelligence required by the raid or TRAP personnel force commander who will execute that mission.

A second major difference between intelligence support to planning and intelligence support to execution is the time available for developing the intelligence product. Often days, weeks, and sometimes months are available to provide intelligence support to planning, but intelligence support to execution must normally be developed in hours, minutes or even seconds. Success in execution often depends on the ability to provide immediate answers to critical questions concerning threat force dispositions, actions, and intentions.

Finally, the uncertainty and disorder that are inherent in the nature of war manifest themselves primarily during execution. Once execution begins, interaction between the opposing wills of friendly and enemy forces normally causes significant and fundamental changes in the situation. Discerning environmental conditions and enemy capabilities and intentions becomes increasingly difficult once these forces are set in motion. Yet it is at precisely this time that commanders require detailed and accurate intelligence to help cope with the uncertainty.

The combined factors of the extensive nature of the IRs, the degree of detail required, the limited time available, and the uncertainty inherent during execution make providing intelligence support to execution the most significant intelligence challenge. Intelligence operations must be prepared to meet this challenge and to provide the flexibility and agility required to deliver continuous situational awareness, identify opportunities, and facilitate rapid decisionmaking.

Intelligence support during execution focuses on providing the commander with practical knowledge that gives an exploitable advantage over the enemy. Although eliminating uncertainty during execution is impossible, focused intelligence operations can reduce uncertainty by providing situational awareness and identifying opportunities as they present themselves in the battlespace. Intelligence provides I&W of new or unexpected enemy activities, enhances efforts to engage the enemy through support to targeting, assists in protecting the force through CI measures and operations, and supports the planning of future operations by providing timely and accurate BDA. Three key factors for ensuring effective intelligence support during execution are resource allocation, linkage to operations, and generation of tempo.

Resource Allocation

Since IRs will always exceed available intelligence resources, intelligence operations must focus where they can have the greatest effect. A detailed and well-thought-out concept of intelligence support, developed in accordance with the commander's intent and concept of operations, will provide an appropriate allocation of intelligence capabilities between the main effort and supporting efforts. It is particularly important that Marine Corps forces (MARFOR), MAGTF, and major subordinate commands (MSCs) who control the tasking of intelligence units and capabilities provide access to critical intelligence resources for their subordinate elements. Those intelligence resources best suited to satisfying current, tactical, mission-specific IRs, such as unmanned aerial vehicles (UAVs) or terrain analysts, should be allocated to units responsible for executing the mission.

Linkage to Operations

To provide effective support to execution, intelligence operations must be linked to planned and ongoing operational activity. Intelligence operations are conducted based on the results of the IPB process, wargaming, and the planning process. Collection, production, and dissemination plans are developed to support execution of specific tactical options, engagement of targets, and selecting branches and sequels to the operation plan. Intelligence personnel must have continuous awareness of planned and ongoing operations to monitor potential enemy reactions, identify new opportunities, and assess the effects of actions on the enemy. Close and continuous synchronization of intelligence activities and operations is essential to developing timely, tailored, and relevant intelligence that facilitates rapid decisionmaking and exploitating opportunities in the battlespace.

GENERATION OF TEMPO

Intelligence operations during execution must facilitate the generation of tempo. First, intelligence operations generate tempo through prioritization. By focusing intelligence operations on satisfying PIRs and supporting the main effort, intelligence is developed that is directly linked to the commander's intent and C2 effort. Next, intelligence facilitates tempo by supporting the decisionmaking process. Intelligence that provides situational awareness and the ability to recognize emerging patterns enables the commander to employ intuitive decisionmaking to make rapid decisions that help generate tempo. Finally, intelligence facilitates tempo by providing knowledge—key elements of data and information that have been analyzed, synthesized, and placed in context to help provide situational awareness—not just a mass of unprocessed information or unrelated pieces of data. The critical factor is not the amount of information provided, but key, focused intelligence that is available when needed and in a useful form that improves the commander's knowledge of the hostile situation and his ability to act. Intelligence operations must have the flexibility, agility, and responsiveness to rapidly collect and process relevant information, develop a focused product, and deliver that product to the affected commander in an easily understandable form and in time for the commander to take appropriate action.

Chapter - 3

Developing Intelligence

Intelligence is developed through the use of the intelligence cycle. This process consists of a sequence of related activities that translate requirements for various types of information into intelligence that is furnished to the commander for use in the decisionmaking cycle. During this sequence, intelligence needs are identified; a *plan* is formulated and *directions* are given for satisfying those needs, data is *collected, processed, and exploited* for usable information then transformed into a tailored, useful intelligence product that is *disseminated* to and *utilized* by the appropriate commander or unit. This process is called the intelligence cycle. At the same time, a parallel process is used to develop CI plans and measures that deny information to an adversary to protect our forces and help ensure the effectiveness of our operations.

Figure 3-1 shows the six steps of the Marine Corps intelligence cycle. These steps define a sequential and interdependent process for the development of intelligence. Intelligence operations are conducted within the framework of the intelligence cycle; the entire cycle or a specific step within the cycle may be the focus of a particular intelligence activity. Moreover, *all* intelligence, regardless of the scope of the requirement or level of command, is developed by following these steps. (See figures 3-2 and 3-3)

No single phase of the cycle is more important than the others. All of the phases are interdependent. Without proper direction, the other phases will not focus on the correct objectives.

Without effective collection, there may be too much or too little information and what information there is may prove to be irrelevant. Without processing and production, there is a mass of random data instead of the knowledge needed for the planning and execution of operations. Intelligence is meaningless unless it reaches the right people in time to affect the decisionmaking process and in an understandable form.

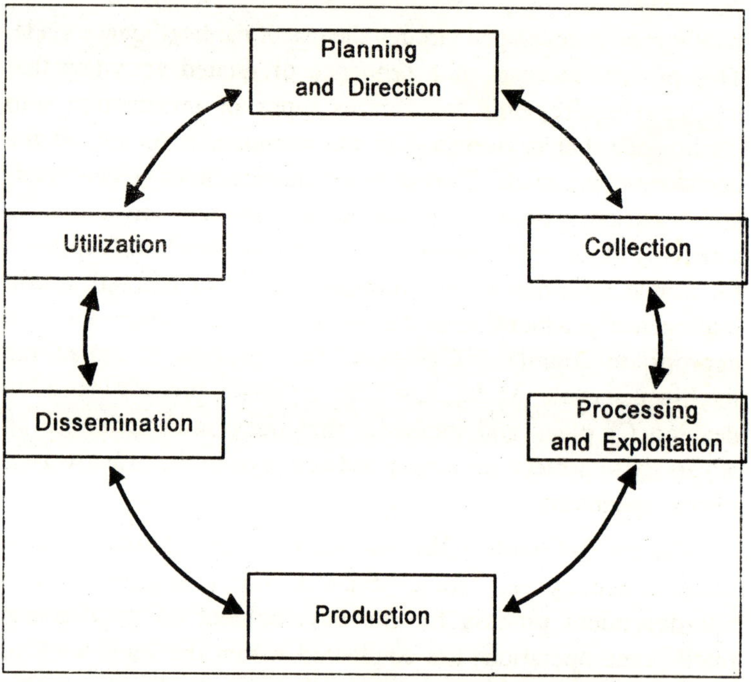

Figure 3-1. *The Marine Corps Intelligence Cycle.*

An understanding of the process used to develop intelligence is critical to the execution of successful intelligence operations. All personnel involved in the *development* and *use* of intelligence must be aware of their role in the process. They must understand the relationship between the steps in the process to ensure that intelligence focuses on the mission and facilitates rapid decisionmaking in the execution of successful combat operations. (See figure 3-4.)

INTELLIGENCE REQUIREMENTS

An intelligence requirement (IR) is a requirement for intelligence to fill a gap in the command's knowledge and understanding of the battlespace or enemy forces.

IRs *drive* the intelligence cycle. Properly articulated, mission-oriented requirements focus the intelligence effort and provide the foundation for successful intelligence operations.

The Intelligence Cycle — Macro View

During a routine review of the situation in the Marine Expeditionary Force's (MEF's) area of interest, the G-2 notes that a recent change in government in one of the countries has created the potential for instability over the next year. The G-2 directs the development of an intelligence estimate to support potential contingency operations in this country. Working with the Marine Corps force G-2 section and the pertinent combatant command's joint intelligence center, the MEF collections section submits requests for imagery intelligence (IMINT), signals intelligence (SIGINT), and HUMINT support. As information is received, the MEF G-2 section's all source fusion platoon (AFP), with the assistance of the topographic platoon, the imagery intelligence platoon (IIP), and the radio battalion, processes and exploits the information to produce the estimate and supporting studies. The estimate is completed within a month. The G-2 directs that copies be forwarded to all major subordinate commands (MSCs) and staff sections, with priority to the forward-deployed MEU. The G-2 also recommends to the commanding general that the scenario for the MEF's upcoming command post (CP) exercise be based on this estimate to introduce MEF personnel to this contingency area, identify planning requirements, and develop potential COAs. The MEF G-2 has *directed* the development of a comprehensive intelligence product that is focused on an operational requirement. Extensive organic capabilities as well as external resources were integrated to *collect* data, *process* it into information, and *produce* the finished intelligence. The product was then *disseminated* to and *utilized* by the units and staff sections with contingency responsibility for the identified area. The intelligence formulated focuses on the mission and facilitates rapid decisionmaking in the execution of successful combat operations.

Figure 3-2. *The Intelligence Cycle—Micro View*

An IR is a missing piece of information about the enemy or environment that a commander needs to know to make a sound decision. In its simplest form, an IR is a question about the threat or the battlespace, the answer to which is required for the planning and execution of an operation.

Examples follow:

- Will the highway bridge support assault amphibious vehicles?
- Will weather conditions interfere with planned air operations?
- Are port facilities and conditions suitable for a maritime prepositioning force pierside offload?
- Can the enemy air defence system threaten low-flying helicopters?
- What is the reaction time of the enemy garrison located south of the amphibious objective area?

Requirements fall into two categories: IRs and PIRs. PIRs and IRs replace the terms essential elements of information and IRs.

The Intelligence Cycle—Micro View

The regiment S-2 section receives a report from one of their reconnaissance teams that an enemy artillery battery has just passed their observation post (OP) and turned off the road. Knowing that enemy artillery is the top targeting priority, the intelligence watch immediately begins developing the target. The S-2 chief checks the map and notes that there are three potential firing positions (identified through the IPB process) close to, but out of visual range of, the reconnaissance OP. The S-2 chief also knows that UAVs are in direct support of the regiment at this time. The S-2 chief alerts the fire support coordination center (FSCC) concerning the potential target and works with the FSCC and air officer to divert an ongoing UAV mission to search the potential firing positions. The UAV quickly locates the enemy artillery in the second firing position. The S-2 chief confirms that the enemy weapons can range friendly positions and, based on their observed activity, are preparing to attack. Using this intelligence, the FSCC coordinates a counterfire mission against the enemy artillery. The S-2 chief successfully executed the intelligence cycle in a matter of minutes. He understood the requirement to develop targeting information, directed the *collection* of information, *processed* the information and *produced* the desired intelligence, that is, a target, and *disseminated* that target to the FSCC, who *utilized* that intelligence to engage the target.

Figure 3-3. *The Intelligence Cycle—Micro View.*

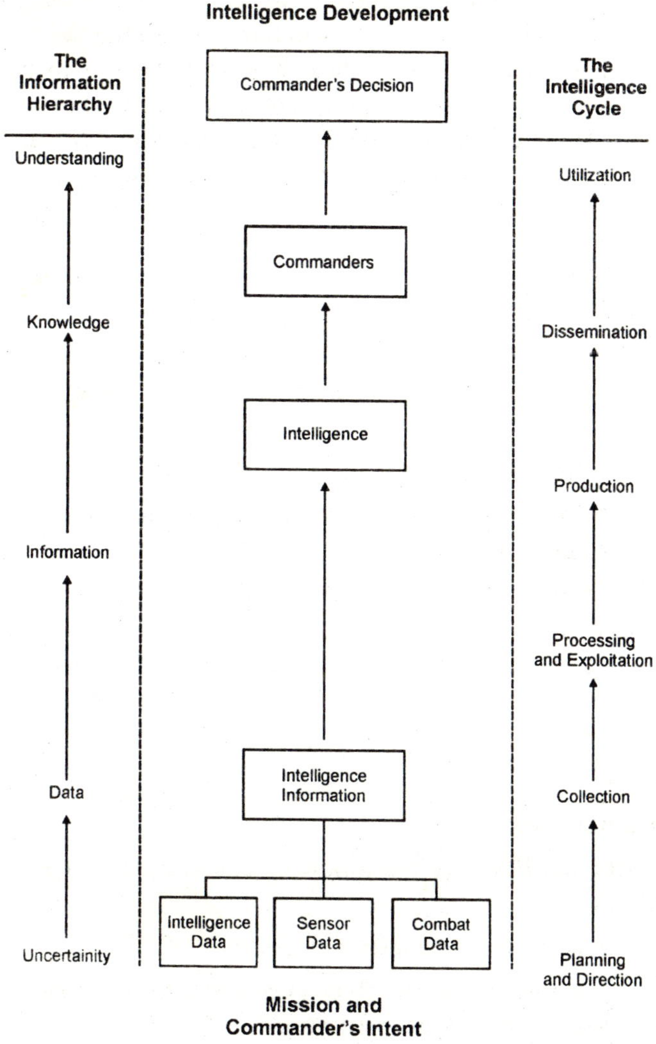

Figure 3-4. *Intelligence Development and the Intelligence Cycle.*

PRIORITY INTELLIGENCE REQUIREMENT

A PIR is an intelligence requirement associated with a decision that will critically affect the overall success of the command's mission.

IRs cover the entire spectrum of information that is needed concerning the battlespace and the threat. The scarce intelligence assets and limited time available will rarely permit the satisfaction of all of a command's IRs; thus, it is important to focus the intelligence effort on those requirements that are critical to mission success. These critical IRs are designated as PIRs. PIRs are the subset of the CCIRs that focus on the threat and the environment. CCIRs are intelligence and information requirements the satisfaction of which the commander deems critical to decisionmaking and mission success. PIRs are linked to specific decisions and, in effect, constitute the commander's guidance for intelligence. Notional PIRs follow:

- What size force is defending amphibious force objective B?
- Which bridges over the Sand River are intact?
- Will the enemy use chemical weapons against the beach support area on D-day?

There is no standard list or set rule for determining PIRs. Each tactical situation poses distinct problems and specific gaps in intelligence. However, the commander will often have PIRs that concern the most likely enemy COA, the most dangerous enemy COA, and critical enemy vulnerabilities that can be exploited.

Characteristics

PIRs and IRs have the following characteristics. Each PIR or IR—

- Asks only one question.
- Focuses on specific facts, events or activities concerning the enemy or the battlespace.
- Is tied to mission planning, decisionmaking, and execution.

- Provides a clear, concise statement of what intelligence is required.
- Contains geographic and time elements to limit the scope of the requirement.

Requirements may be simple or complex. It is important to understand that the nature and scope of PIRs and IRs will vary with the mission and the level of command, and on the particular phase in the PDE&A cycle. Requirements will generally become more focused as the intelligence cycle is executed. During execution, the intelligence effort should be directed against a small number of PIRs that are closely linked to the concept of operations.

PLANNING AND DIRECTION

The planning and direction phase of the intelligence cycle consists of those activities that identify pertinent IRs and provide the means for satisfying those requirements. (See figure 3-5.) Intelligence planning and direction is a continuous function and a command responsibility. The commander directs the intelligence effort. The intelligence officer manages this effort for the commander based on the intent, designation of PIRs, and specific guidance provided during the planning process.

Requirements Development
Requirements Management
Collection Management
Production Management
Dissemination Management

Figure 3-5. *Planning and Direction Phase Functions.*

REQUIREMENTS DEVELOPMENT

Identification of Requirements

Concise, mission-oriented IRs provide clear direction to the intelligence effort. The entire staff and all subordinate commanders play a role in developing the command's IRs. The intelligence officer formulates most of the initial requirements by using the original mission tasking together with knowledge of the threat, familiarity with the operating area, and experience derived from participation in the commander's decisionmaking process to anticipate the majority of the basic intelligence needs. As the planning process continues, the commander, other staff officers, and subordinate commands expand on previously identified requirements and develop new ones. Requirements are generally linked to proposed COAs or potential decisions. The intelligence officer records, collates, and refines these requirements as they are identified and maintains a consolidated list of requirements.

Designation of PIRs

The commander makes a critical contribution to the intelligence effort by designating the PIRs. As COAs and supporting information requirements are developed, the satisfaction of certain IRs will be essential to mission success. The identification of these "show stoppers" forms the basis for designating PIRs. The intelligence officer, with input from other members of the staff, draws up a recommended list of PIRs. PIRs will be listed in priority order relative to their importance to mission accomplishment. In forming this list, the G-2/S-2 considers the requirements of his own command, subordinate commands, adjacent commands, and any direction received from higher headquarters. Recommendations are submitted to the commander who reviews, refines, and approves the command's PIRs. In designating PIRs, the commander establishes the following:

- What he wants to know (intelligence required).
- Why he wants it (linked to operational decisionmaking).
- When he needs it (latest time that the information will be of value).
- How he wants it (format, method of delivery).

Once approved and distributed, PIRs constitute the core of the commander's guidance for the intelligence process.

REQUIREMENTS MANAGEMENT

Management of IRs is a dynamic process that encompasses the continuous evaluation of the following:

- Importance of each requirement to mission success.
- Information and assets needed to satisfy each requirement.
- Resources that are presently committed toward fulfilling that requirement.
- Degree that the requirement has been satisfied by completed intelligence activities.

Processing Requirements

Developing requirements and designating PIRs are not one-time efforts. There is a dynamic flow of new requirements, existing requirements are satisfied or no longer relevant, and the relative importance of each requirement changes as the PDE&A cycle progresses. (See figure 3-6.) As requirements are developed, the intelligence officer validates, refines, and enters them into the management system.

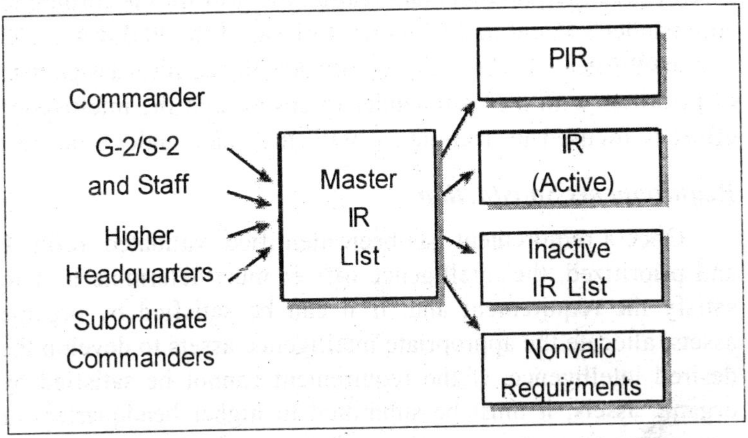

Figure 3-6. *Intelligence Requirements Management.*

Validation ensures that the requirement is relevant to the mission, has not already been satisfied, and does not duplicate other requirements.

Refining the requirement entails placing it in the proper format, identifying all information components related to the requirement, and adding appropriate qualifiers such as geographic limitations or time constraints. During refinement, similar or related requirements may be combined into a single, comprehensive requirement.

A requirements management system is an essential tool that provides means to monitor the effort to satisfy each requirement. Each intelligence section must develop a system appropriate to its mission and echelon. Minimal components of any system are a numbering system, identification of who submitted the requirement, designation of collection and production resources committed to satisfying the requirement (or noting when it was submitted to higher headquarters or supporting forces, if organic assets are not available), timeliness requirements, dissemination instructions and information, and a mechanism to ensure user satisfaction.

Determining Priorities

The intelligence officer must continually reassess the emphasis given to each requirement and realign the priorities according to commander's intent and the current phase of the PDE&A cycle. The intelligence officer must also periodically confirm assignment of priorities with the commander to ensure that the intelligence effort is focused in accordance with the commander's desires.

Requirements Satisfaction

Once a requirement has been identified, validated, refined, and prioritized, the intelligence officer must determine how to satisfy the requirement and, if it can be satisfied by organic assets, allocate the appropriate intelligence assets to develop the desired intelligence. If the requirement cannot be satisfied by organic assets, it must be submitted to higher headquarters or supporting forces/agencies for satisfaction. In determining how to satisfy a requirement, the intelligence officer must consider each step in the intelligence cycle to ensure that the plan encompasses the entire process from collection through utilization.

The intelligence offieer must identify the information needed, where and how to get it, how to package the intelligence into an appropriate product, and how to deliver that product. Normally, an IR will generate a requirement to do the following:

- Collect data or information.
- Process and produce intelligence in the scope and form that answers the question.
- Disseminate the information to a particular user by a specific time. (See figure 3-7.)

Directing the Intelligence Effort

Intelligence direction consists of the requirements development and management process described above combined

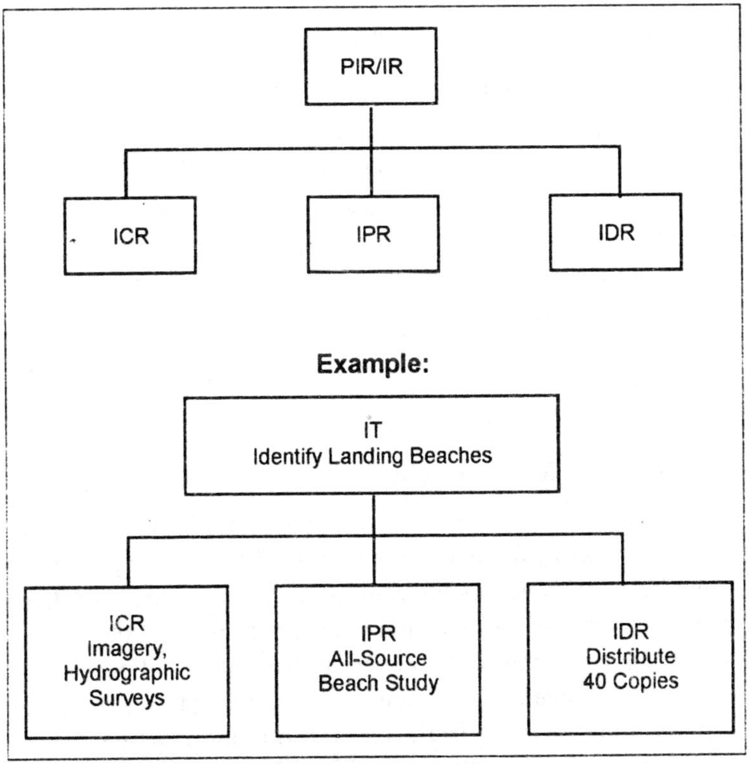

Figure 3-7. *Requirements Satisfaction.*

with the associated functions of collection management, production management, and dissemination management. Because the possible questions about the enemy and the AO are practically infinite but intelligence assets are limited, the intelligence effort must be managed at each step in the process. Management of requirements, collection, production, and dissemination ensures that the effort is focused on the PIRs and delivers knowledge that facilitates sound tactical decisionmaking.

Collection Management

Collection management is the process of converting IRs into collection requirements, establishing priorities, tasking or coordinating with appropriate collection sources or agencies, monitoring results, and retasking, as required. Its purpose is to conduct an effective effort to collect all necessary data while ensuring the efficient use of limited and valuable collection assets.

Production Management

Production management encompasses determining the scope, content, and format of each product; developing a plan and schedule for the development of each product; assigning priorities among the various intelligence production requirements; allocating processing, exploitation, and production resources; and integrating production efforts with collection and dissemination. As with collection management, the goal is to make effective and efficient use of limited resources and ensure that the production effort is properly focused on established priorities.

Dissemination Management

Dissemination management involves establishing dissemination priorities, selecting dissemination means, and monitoring the flow of intelligence throughout the command. Its objective is to deliver the required intelligence to the appropriate user in the proper form at the right time while ensuring that individual consumers and the dissemination system are not overloaded by attempting to move unneeded or irrelevant information. Dissemination management also provides support for use of security controls that do not impede the timely delivery or subsequent use of intelligence while protecting intelligence sources and methods.

Planning the Intelligence Support System

This activity includes designing and establishing the structure that is necessary to provide intelligence support throughout the course of an operation. The intelligence officer looks at the entire body of IRs rather than at individual IRs or PIRs. The intelligence officer anticipates the continuing intelligence needs of the force as it carries out its mission and designs an intelligence support system that has the capability, flexibility, and redundancy to satisfy these needs. After the support system concept is developed, the resources needed to build the system are identified, requested, and acquired. Factors taken into consideration during this effort follow:

- Task organization of intelligence units.
- Identification of personnel and equipment requirements.
- Requirement for liaison teams.
- Connectivity with national, theater, joint, and multinational force intelligence assets.
- Communications and information systems (CIS) requirements.
- Logistic requirements.
- The need for specialized capabilities; e.g., linguists.

COLLECTION

Collection is the gathering of intelligence data and information to satisfy the identified requirements. The collection phase encompasses assembling relevant information from sources that are already on hand or available from other intelligence organizations: intelligence databases, studies, maps, and a workbook or situation map. Collection consists of the activities of organic, attached, and supporting intelligence collection assets to gather new data and deliver it to the appropriate processing or production agency; i.e., the execution of collection operations. Functions carried out during the execution of collection operations follow:

- Mission planning.
- Positioning of assets to locations that are favorable to satisfying collection objectives.
- Data collection.
- Reporting.
- Supervision of individual collection missions.

Radio Battalion
Force Reconnaissance Company
Marine Tactical Electronic Warfare Squadron (VMAQ)
Marine UAV Squadron (VMU)
Ground Sensor Platoon (GSP)
Division Reconnaissance Battalion
CI/HUMINT Company
Light Armoured Reconnaissance Battalion

Figure 3-8. *MAGTF Primary Organic Collection Assets.*

Intelligence data and information are collected by a variety of intelligence assets, each with unique capabilities and limitations.

The value of a collection source is not necessarily related to the sophistication or cost of that source, but rather to its ability to gather pertinent data from the collection target—the enemy or environmental consideration that is the subject of the particular intelligence collection requirement. Successful intelligence operations require access to data from all types of collection resources: organic, joint, national, and multinational. Collection operations are executed to gather data from all suitable and capable assets, balancing the capabilities of one type of collector against the limitations of another to provide "all-source" data input to the processing and exploitation and production phases.

The primary types of intelligence data used to produce tactical intelligence are described in the following paragraphs.

Imagery Intelligence

Imagery intelligence is intelligence derived from the exploitation of collection by visual photography, infrared sensors, lasers, electro-optics, and radar sensors such as synthetic aperture radar wherein images of objects are reproduced optically or electronically on film, electronic display devices, or other media.

Principal sources of imagery are national overhead reconnaissance systems; manned aircraft such as the F-14 or F/A-18 with the Advanced Tactical Airborne Reconnaissance System, the U-2 or the Joint Surveillance Target Attack Radar System; and UAVs. IMINT provides concrete, detailed, and precise information on the location and physical characteristics of the environment and the threat. It is the primary source of information concerning key terrain features, installations, and infrastructure used to build detailed intelligence studies and target materials. The main limitation of IMINT is the time required to task, collect, process, and analyze the imagery. Detailed planning and coordination is required to ensure that the results of imagery collection missions are received in time to affect the decisionmaking process. Imagery operations can be hampered by weather, the enemy's air defence capability, and his camouflage, cover, and deception activities.

Signals Intelligence

SIGINT is intelligence information derived from the interception, processing, and analysis of foreign communications, noncommunications electronic emissions, and instrumentation signals. SIGINT is provided by the radio battalion; the Marine tactical electronic warfare squadron; and an integrated network of national, theater, and joint force SIGINT support agencies. SIGINT provides timely and accurate data on enemy forces that may include details on enemy composition, identification, and location. It can also give insight into the enemy's current status and activities and future intentions. SIGINT is one of the primary means for providing I&W of enemy actions. It is also a principal contributor to intelligence support to IO through its analysis and exploitation of the enemy's C2 system. Principal limitations of SIGINT are that the enemy must transmit signals that can be exploited and that collection assets must be capable of intercepting and positioned to intercept those signals.

Human Intelligence

HUMINT is a category of intelligence derived from information collected and provided by human sources.

HUMINT operations cover a wide range of activities, including reconnaissance patrols, aircrew reports and debriefs, debriefing of refugees, and interrogations of enemy prisoners of war. Principal dedicated HUMINT resources are ground reconnaissance units; the CI and interrogator translator assets of the MEF CI/HUMINT company; and national, theater, and other Service HUMINT elements. All Marines participating in an operation can obtain significant information about the threat and environment. Intelligence operations must aggressively employ Marines as HUMINT sources by teaching them the importance of observing and reporting.

HUMINT can provide insight into intangible factors such as tactics, training, morale, and combat effectiveness that cannot be collected by technical means and offers the best potential source to discern future plans and intentions. HUMINT is particularly important in MOOTW, in which the nature of the mission and of the threat generally provide a lucrative environment for HUMINT operations.

HUMINT has two main limitations as follows:

- HUMINT operations generally require placing humans at risk to gain access to their targets. For that reason, IRs should be satisfied through technical collection means, if possible, before considering the use of human resources.

- HUMINT responsiveness can be limited in certain circumstances because of the time it takes to plan the activities, position the assets, collect the data from what are often hostile or noncooperative sources, and report the information to exploitation and production centers, which are often located a significant distance from the collection site.

Measurement and Signature Intelligence

Measurement and signature intelligence (MASINT) is intelligence information gathered by technical instruments such as radars, passive electro-optical sensors, radiation detectors, and remote ground sensors. Although the primary tactical application of these devices is to collect sensor data, which is generally provided directly to operation centers for immediate decisionmaking, the data collected can also provide significant intelligence information on enemy movements and activities. Key MAGTF MASINT capabilities are remote ground sensors, weapons locating radars, and air surveillance radars. These sensors provide an efficient means to maintain surveillance over large portions of the battlespace. Their limitations include the logistic support required to maintain the equipment, the requirement to place the sensors in proximity to the surveillance area, and the exploitable electronic signatures associated with some of the sensors.

Open-Source Intelligence

Open-source intelligence (OSINT) is information of potential intelligence value that is available to the general public.

OSINT sources include books, magazines, newspapers, maps, commercial electronic networks and databases, and radio and television broadcasts. OSINT involves no information that is classified at its origin or acquired through controlled collection. National and theater intelligence production centers have access to a range of OSINT sources. MAGTF intelligence agencies can receive OSINT through these centers in addition to collecting information from open sources that are available in the AO. OSINT can be a valuable source of geographic, political, economic, sociological, and cultural information, particularly in security, humanitarian assistance or peace operations. In multinational operations, OSINT provides intelligence that can be readily shared with members of a multinational force. However, the sources of OSINT should be carefully evaluated to determine the accuracy and reliability of the information provided.

Counterintelligence

CI is the intelligence function concerned with identifying and counteracting the threat posed by foreign intelligence capabilities and by organizations or individuals engaged in espionage, sabotage, subversion or terrorism. The principal objective of CI is to assist with protecting DOD personnel, family members, resources, facilities, and critical infrastructure. CI provides critical intelligence support to command force protection efforts by helping identify potential threats, threat capabilities, and planned intentions to friendly operations while helping deceive the adversary as to friendly capabilities, vulnerabilities, and intentions. CI increases uncertainty for the enemy, thereby making a significant contribution to the success of friendly operations. CI also identifies friendly vulnerabilities, evaluates security measures, and assists with implementing appropriate security plans. The integration of other intelligence disciplines, CI, and operations culminates .n a cohesive unit force protection programme.

Processing and Exploitation

Processing and exploitation involves the conversion of collected data into information that is suitable for the production of intelligence. Processing is largely a technical function that does not add meaning to the data but that is necessary to convert the data into a form that people can understand. Examples of processing include developing a piece of film, translating a document or communications intercept from a foreign language or converting electronic data into a standardized report that can be analyzed by a system operator. Some types of data require minimal processing. They may be collected in a form that is already suitable for production. Processing may also take place automatically during collection. Other types of data require extensive processing, which can affect the timeliness and accuracy of the resulting information.

Data may be further exploited to gain the fullest possible advantage. For example, an aerial photograph or a frame of UAV video may be exploited by imagery interpreters to identify specific pieces of equipment or measure the dimensions of structures found on that image. When resources are required to accomplish the processing and exploitation phase, it is crucial that processing requirements be prioritized and managed according to the PIRs to ensure that critical information is extracted first.

PRODUCTION

Production is the activity that converts information into intelligence. It involves the evaluation, interpretation, integration, analysis, and synthesis of all information that is relevant to a particular IR to answer the question that has been asked. Production fuses new information and existing intelligence from all sources to provide meaningful knowledge that can be applied to the decisionmaking process. During the production phase, information is—

- Evaluated to determine pertinence, reliability, and accuracy.
- Analyzed to isolate significant elements.
- Integrated with other relevant information and previously developed intelligence.
- Interpreted to form logical conclusions that bears on the situation and supports the commander's decisionmaking process.
- Applied to estimate possible outcomes.

- Placed into the product format that will be most useful to its eventual user.

Intelligence Preparation of the Battlespace

IPB is the primary analytical methodology used to produce intelligence in support of the decisionmaking process. It furnishes a framework for integrating intelligence and operations throughout the PDE&A cycle. IPB is a systematic, continuous, mission-focused process of analyzing the environment and the threat in a specific geographic area.

Define the Battlespace Environment
Describe the Battlespace Effects
Evaluate the Adversary
Determine Adversary COAs

Figure 3-9. *Intelligence Preparation of the Battlespace.*

IPB provides a means to interpret information and understand the battlespace that can be applied in any operational situation. Through the IPB process, information that has been collected and processed is analyzed, synthesized, and used to estimate possible outcomes that can affect mission accomplishment. The result is knowledge based intelligence that is incorporated into a variety of intelligence products.

Although IPB is fundamentally an intelligence process, successful application of the process to support planning and execution depends on the participation of the commander and the entire staff. The commander is responsible for intelligence production and IPB. The commander focuses the IPB effort by defining the area and key factors to be studied. The commander's guidance and the complete involvement of the staff are necessary to ensure that the IPB effort encompasses aspects of concern for all warfighting functions and provides detailed and accurate intelligence for COA development and detailed planning. Finally, the commander ensures that the IPB process is fully integrated with mission planning and execution. IPB is an effective tool only when the results are used to develop plans and support decisionmaking during execution.

IPB emphasizes providing intelligence in the form of graphics and images—formats that help the commander to rapidly visualize, assimilate, and apply the intelligence in the decisionmaking process. During planning, products generated from IPB place large volumes of intelligence in context, providing situational awareness for everyone involved in the planning effort. These products form the basis of, or are combined with, the planning tools and decision support aids prepared by other staff sections to provide an integrated planning and execution support product. During execution, the use of graphics display intelligence increases the commander's ability to discern patterns as they are emerging and to conduct intuitive decisionmaking, thereby increasing operational tempo.

Levels of Production

Intelligence production can be extremely simple or incredibly complex. At the MAGTF CE level, particularly during deliberate planning, production normally entails developing detailed, allsource estimates and studies through the combined efforts of several intelligence support elements. During tactical execution, time constraints and the demands of the ongoing battle require rapid processing and production, with an emphasis on developing simple, mission focused intelligence products such as a hand annotated image of a helicopter landing zone (HLZ), a target description or an overlay depicting current and future enemy dispositions. An enlisted intelligence specialist on duty in an infantry battalion command post may develop dozens of intelligence products during his watch in the form of answers to questions concerning the enemy situation, targets or terrain to be traversed. Valuable intelligence does not result solely from the investment of time or resources. It is developed by placing relevant information in context, converting it into knowledge through analysis and synthesis, and applying that knowledge to the decisionmaking process.

There is inherent friction between the desire to provide as complete and accurate an intelligence product as possible and the continuous requirement to support the time-sensitive urgency of tactical decisionmaking. In practice, these conflicting demands must be balanced by using stated direction, such as the commander's intent and PIRs, and knowledge of the operational situation to determine when to finish and disseminate the product. To provide a framework to make these determinations, intelligence production can be viewed as occurring on two levels: deliberate and immediate.

Deliberate production is employed when there is sufficient time to thoroughly evaluate, analyze, and synthesize all available information and produce a formal intelligence product such as a written intelligence estimate, scheduled report or detailed target/objective area study.

Immediate production is conducted to identify, process, and place in context elements of data, information, and intelligence that have a direct effect on ongoing or near-term operations. These elements are subjected to a compressed version of the production process, and the resulting product is rapidly disseminated to those who are affected. Immediate production is normally conducted during execution and results in simple, mission-specific intelligence products: situational assessments or answers to specific, individual IRs. There is no absolute distinction between the two levels. The nature of the situation and pertinent IRs will dictate the amount of time available to complete each production effort. Likewise, IPB methodology should be used during both types of production. However, during immediate production, a rapid mental evaluation and integration of the relevant factors of the threat and environment are used, usually building on a deliberate production effort that has already been completed.

DISSEMINATION

Dissemination is the timely conveyance of intelligence to users in an appropriate form. Many times, intelligence operations focus almost exclusively on the collection and production phases, with the intelligence cycle often breaking down because insufficient attention is given to the dissemination phase. Dissemination must be planned and supervised to the same degree as collection and production or we risk failure of the intelligence support function. Determining the form and selection of the means to deliver the product are key aspects of the dissemination process.

Form

Determining the form to be used in disseminating the intelligence product is a function of several factors: the purpose of the intelligence product, the urgency and relevance of the intelligence to ongoing operations, the type and volume of the intelligence, the user's capability to receive intelligence products, and the dissemination means available. Because decisionmaking is a mental process and human beings think and understand primarily in the form of images, the goal of intelligence dissemination is to convey an accurate image of the battlespace or threat to the decisionmaker in a form that facilitates rapid understanding of that image. For this reason, graphics are the preferred dissemination form. (See figure 3-10 and figure 3-11)

Although oral briefings and written reports are the primary dissemination forms used today, the use of automated systems is increasing the capability to develop graphic products. Imagery, overlays, diagrams, and schematics enhanced with appropriate textual data and annotations will be used as the baseline dissemination format whenever possible. However, in time-sensitive situations, the verbal report or short text message may be the most expeditious dissemination form. Whether oral, text or graphic, intelligence products should use standard formats whenever possible. Standard formats facilitate ease of preparation and dissemination, as well as usability of the intelligence product.

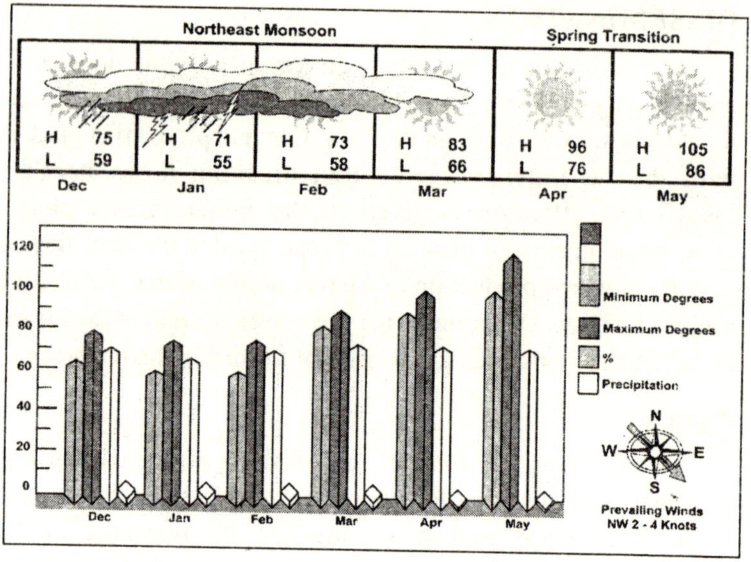

Figure 3-10. *Graphic Climatology Study.*

Delivery

Delivery of the intelligence product to the right person in a timely manner is directly related to the choice of the means used to disseminate that product. Dissemination is managed by using a combination of methods, channels, and modes to convey the product to the user.

Methods

There are two basic methods used to disseminate intelligence: supply-push and demand-pull. A supply-push system pushes intelligence from the collectors/producers to the users as it becomes available. The main advantage to this method is that users do not have to initiate requests to receive products. However, there is potential for information overload in a supply-push system. To prevent information overload, the dissemination node should tailor what it is passing through the system, not simply dump everything that it has received or developed.

The demand-pull mode provides access to intelligence on an as-needed basis. The user draws the required intelligence from the intelligence support system through a series of searches or inquiries. The use of demand-pull decreases the volume of intelligence being transmitted and diminishes the possibility of overwhelming units with superfluous products. However, demand-pull can also reduce the timeliness of dissemination by developing and providing intelligence only after a request has been received.

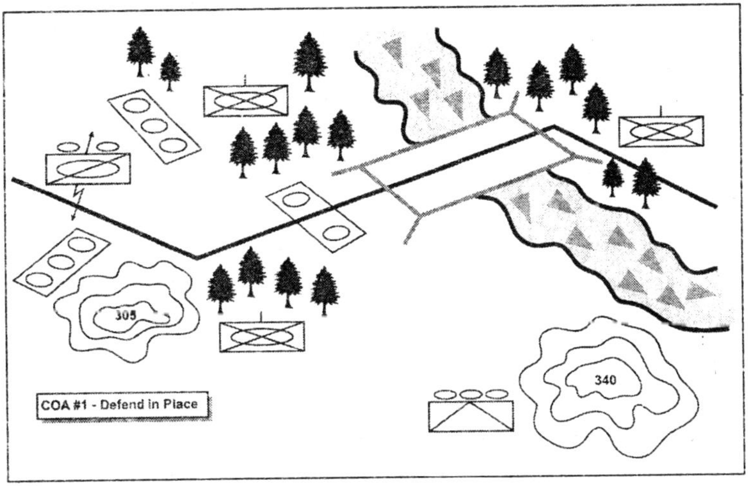

Figure 3-11. *Graphic Intelligence Estimate.*

The dissemination system must provide the flexibility to use either method, "pushing" important or time-sensitive intelligence directly to the users, while at the same time permitting them to "pull" other relevant intelligence as needed from readily accessible sources such as a database or a watch section at an intelligence center.

Channels

Intelligence is disseminated by using two types of channels: *standard* and *alarm*. Standard dissemination is used for routine intelligence and is transmitted according to a set order and format, usually along established command or staff channels. Examples include the formal staff briefing and standardized reports. The alarm channel is used to disseminate critical, time-sensitive intelligence that can have an immediate effect on the conduct of the operation, such as I&W of hostile activity. I&W alarms must be disseminated rapidly to all units that are affected by that intelligence. Although the standard channel is used to satisfy the majority of dissemination requirements, care must be taken to monitor the flow of what is passing through the pipeline to ensure that the intelligence provided is timely and pertinent to the units receiving it. A particularly important connection that is often neglected in standard dissemination is *lateral dissemination*; intelligence must flow laterally between units as well as up and down the chain of command. The exchange of intelligence between the GCE, aviation combat element (ACE), and combat service support element (CSSE) is an especially important link in ensuring that all commanders have a shared picture of the battlespace.

Modes

Finally, intelligence is disseminated in one of two modes: *broadcast* or *point-to-point*. In broadcast dissemination, intelligence that affects the majority of units is sent simultaneously to a broad audience. Examples include I&W alarms, intelligence products developed by the MAGTF G-2 section that support the entire MAGTF, and reporting from organic collection assets. Broadcast dissemination may be web-based. Successful use of the broadcast mode depends on several factors, including judicious selection of what intelligence is broadcast, the ability of the appropriate users to monitor the broadcast, and employment of a processing methodology or system to filter and select for detailed examination only those broadcast items that are pertinent to the user's requirements. Undisciplined use of this mode can quickly lead to information overload. In the point-to-point mode, intelligence is sent to a specific user or users, normally in response to a specific request or requirement, and is passed along sequentially as appropriate. Dissemination across the system is slower but is more focused and can provide intelligence that is tailored to the needs of each individual unit. Point-to-point dissemination may be enhanced through the use of classified e-mail systems.

Architectures

Intelligence architectures provide the means to disseminate intelligence. (See figure 3-12) Dissemination planning analyzes and anticipates the dissemination requirements and designs the appropriate architecture to meet those requirements. The architecture should employ all methods, channels, and modes in a flexible, integrated system. The objective is to provide the right intelligence to the appropriate user in a timely manner, while at the same time not overwhelming him with a massive amount of unfocused data.

Architectures will be developed with the objective of facilitating the exchange of *graphic* intelligence throughout the force, down to the lowest tactical echelon. The means will consist of a combination of procedures, CIS, and communications networks, effectively supervised by intelligence specialists to ensure that the dissemination requirements are being satisfied. The intelligence architecture must be interoperable with the overall CIS architecture employed by the MAGTF and the joint force.

UTILIZATION

Intelligence has no inherent value. Its value is realized through its support to operations. Thus, the intelligence cycle is not complete until the intelligence that has been developed is used in decisionmaking during planning and/or execution. The commander is responsible for the effective use of intelligence and for ensuring that decisions are based on the foundation provided by intelligence. The intelligence officer facilitates the effective use of intelligence, supervises the entire intelligence development effort, and assists the commander and the staff in understanding the intelligence product and its application.

The utilization phase also provides the basis for the continuous functioning of the intelligence cycle. On one hand, utilization will determine whether a requirement has been completely satisfied;

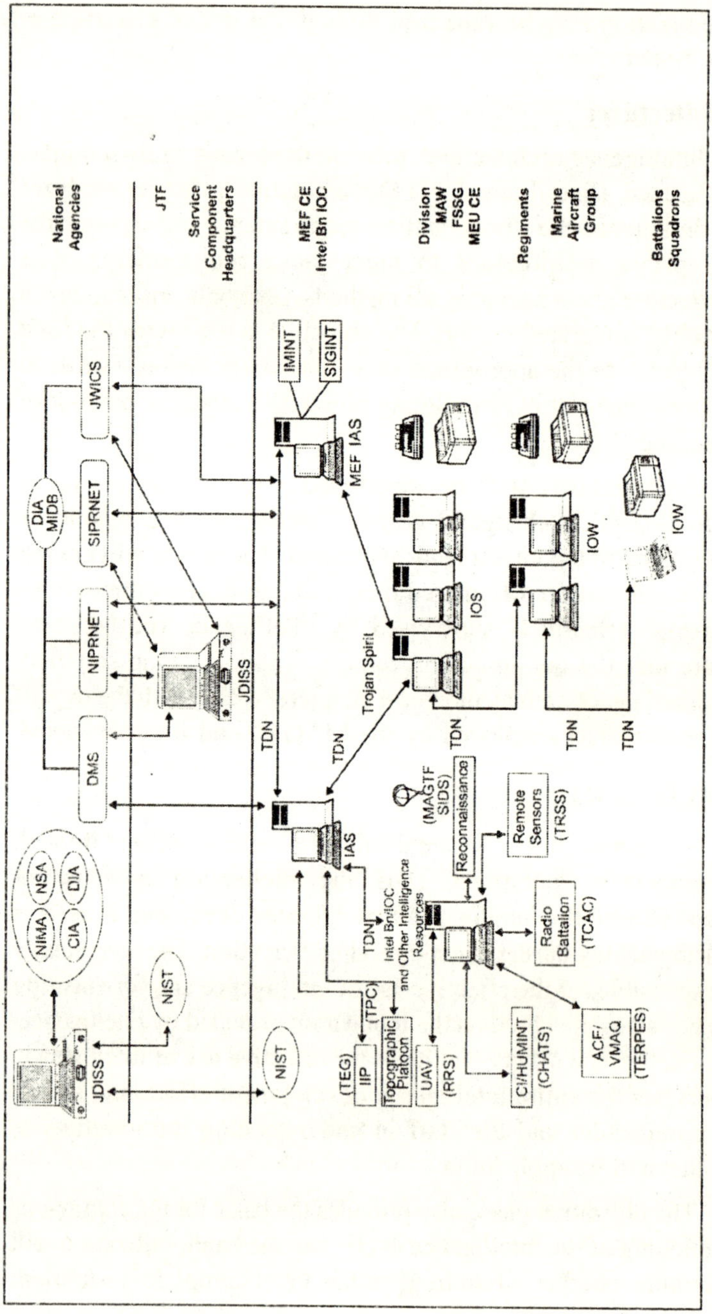

Figure 3-12. *Notional Marine Expeditionary Force Intelligence Architecture.*

CHATS=CI/HUMINT automated tool set
CIA=Central Intelligence Agency
CI/HUMINT=counterintelligence/human intelligence
DIA=Defence Intelligence Agency
DMS=Defence Message System
IAS=Intelligence analysis system
IIP=imagery intelligence platoon
intel bn=intelligence battalion
IOS=intelligence operations server
IOW=intelligence operations workstation
JWICS=Joint Worldwide Intelligence Communication System
MAW FSSG=Marine Aircraft Wing Force Service Support Group (USMC)
MIDB=modernized integrated database
NIMA=National Imagery and Mapping Agency
NIPRNET=Non-Secure Internet Protocol Router Network
NIST=National Intelligence Support Team
NSA=National Security Agency
RRS=remote receive station
SIDS=secondary imagery dissemination system
SIPRNET=Secret Internet Protocol Router Network
TCAC=Technical Control and Analysis Center
TDN=tactical data network
TEG=Technical Exploitation Group
TERPES=tactical electronic reconnaissance processing and evaluation system
TPC=topographic production capability
TRSS=tactical remote sensor system

requirements that have not been met will require additional intelligence development efforts. On the other hand, the satisfaction of one requirement normally generates new or additional requirements, the answers to which are needed to further refine or focus the decisionmaking process. In either case, utilization provides guidance and feedback that are used to initiate the next iteration of the cycle.

APPLICATION OF THE INTELLIGENCE CYCLE

The intelligence cycle is a procedural framework for developing mission-focused intelligence support. It is not an end in itself, nor should it be viewed as a rigid set of procedures that must be carried out in an identical manner on all occasions. The commander and the intelligence officer must consider each IR individually and apply the intelligence cycle in a manner that develops the required intelligence in the most effective way.

Application of the intelligence cycle will vary with the phase of the PDE&A cycle. In theory, a unique iteration of the intelligence cycle is carried out for each individual requirement. In practice, particularly during the planning phase, requirements are grouped together and satisfied through a single, concurrent intelligence development process. During the planning phase, intelligence development is generally carried out through two major iterations of the intelligence cycle.

The first primarily supports decision planning. Completing this iteration of the intelligence cycle results in preparing and using basic intelligence products—an intelligence estimate, supporting studies, and IPB analysis—that describe the battlespace and threat. These products form the basis for developing and selecting COAs.

The second iteration of the intelligence cycle supports execution planning. It is an outgrowth of selecting the COA and forming a concept of operations. Implementing the collection plan, refinement of IPB analysis, and generating mission-specific intelligence products are integrated with the concept of operations to support mission execution. During execution, requirements are satisfied on a more individualized basis. New requirements are usually generated in response to a specific operational need. Each requirement is unique and must be satisfied in a timely manner to facilitate rapid decisionmaking and generating or maintaining tempo. (See figure 3-13)

The intelligence cycle will also be applied differently depending on the mission and the organizational level of the unit. For example, a MAGTF G-2 section will normally have a separate section that is specifically responsible for each phase of the intelligence cycle— collections section, processing and exploitation agencies, a production element, and a dissemination section—with an intelligence operations section providing planning and direction for the overall effort. At the MAGTF level, intelligence is normally developed to satisfy multiple requirements concurrently, with simultaneous collection, processing, production, and utilization

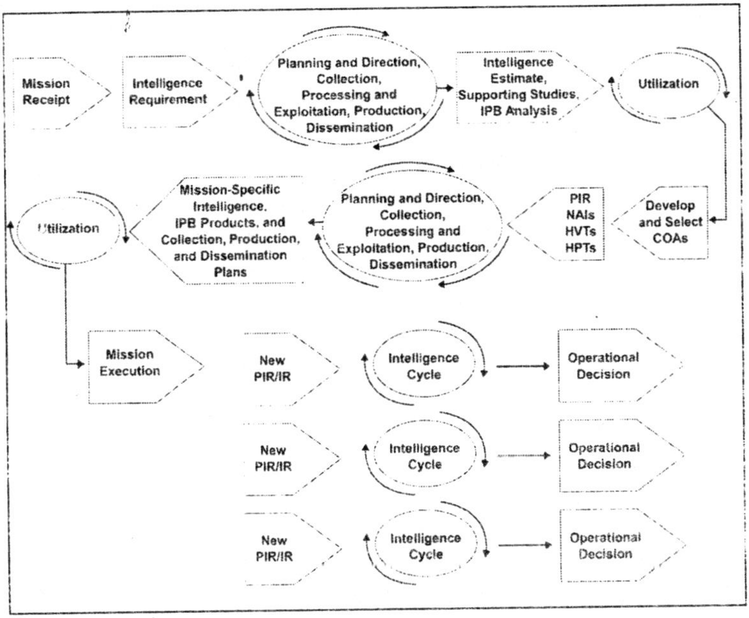

Figure 3-13. *Application of the Intelligence Cycle.*

efforts being carried out by the separate functional sections. In contrast, a battalion or squadron S-2 section must carry out the cycle with a limited number of resources. It will generally focus on a single requirement or a small number of closely related requirements, moving through each phase of the cycle sequentially until that requirement is satisfied.

COUNTERINTELLIGENCE

CI is the function of intelligence that is concerned with identifying and counteracting the threat posed by hostile intelligence capabilities and by organizations or individuals engaged in espionage, sabotage, subversion, or terrorism. The objective of CI is to enhance the security of the command by denying an adversary information that might be used to conduct effective operations against friendly forces and to protect the command by identifying and neutralizing espionage, sabotage, subversion, or terrorism efforts.

Responsibilities

CI, like all intelligence matters, is a command responsibility. In preparing for operations, all units must develop a CI plan and implement appropriate CI measures to protect themselves from potential threats. The unit intelligence officer plans, implements, and supervises the CI effort for the commander. The G-2/S-2 may have access to or request support from MAGTF CI units and specialists to assist in developing CI estimates and plans. All members of the command are involved in executing the CI plan and implementing appropriate CI measures. Key participants in this process and their specific responsibilities follow:

- G-3/S-3-overall security and force protection,
- PSEC, counterreconnaissance, and deception.
- G-6/S-6-CIS security.
- G-1/S-1-information security.
- Headquarters commandant-physical security of unit CP and echelons.

CI Planning

CI planning at all levels is conducted by using a standard methodology that consists of three steps: developing a CI estimate, conducting a CI survey, and developing the CI plan.

The CI Estimate

The CI estimate details the capabilities and limitations of foreign intelligence, subversive, and terrorist organizations that could carry out actions against friendly units and facilities or against individuals, groups or locations of concern to our forces, such as the local population or civilian organizations operating in the area. It also provides an estimate of possible and probable COAs that these threat organizations will adopt. Intelligence and CI analysts of the MAGTF CE and CI/HUMINT company will normally prepare a comprehensive CI estimate that addresses threats to the MARFOR or MAGTF by using an IPB methodology that is focused on CI factors and the CI threat. However. each level of command must conduct its own evaluation to determine which of the adversary's capabilities identified in the MAGTF CI estimate represent a threat to their particular unit. The CI estimate must be updated on a regular basis. The revised estimate or appropriate CI warning reports must be disseminated to all units involved in the operation.

The CI Survey

The CI survey assesses a unit's security posture against the threats detailed in the CI estimate. The CI survey should identify vulnerabilities to specific foreign intelligence, espionage, sabotage, subversion or terrorist capabilities and provide recommendations on how to eliminate or minimize these vulnerabilities. The survey should be as detailed as possible. During the planning phase of an operation, it may be possible to do a formal, written survey. CI specialists from the CI/HUMINT company may be available to assist in this effort. In a time-compressed situation, the survey will likely result from a brief discussion between the appropriate intelligence, operations, communications, and security personnel. In either case, it is critical that the survey look forward in space and time to support developing the CI measures necessary to protect the unit as it carries out successive phases of the operation; i.e., the survey makes recommendations to improve the CI posture of the command for now and in the future.

The CI Plan

The CI plan details the activities and operations that the command will use to counter the CI threat. It includes procedures for detecting and monitoring the activities of foreign intelligence and terrorist organizations and directs the implementation of active and passive measures that are intended to protect the force from these activities. The CI plan is based on the threats identified in the CI estimate and the vulnerabilities detected by the CI survey. The MAGTF staff CI officer normally prepares a detailed, comprehensive CI plan that addresses the entire MAGTF. Included in the MAGTF CI plan are details of the employment of dedicated CI capabilities and the conduct of specialized CI operations intended to detect and neutralize or eliminate specific CI threats. Plans of subordinate MAGTF elements closely follow the MAGTF plan, normally adding only security measures that apply to their specific units. As with all plans, CI plans must be continually updated to ensure they are current and support ongoing and future operations.

CI Measures

CI measures encompass a broad range of activities designed to protect against the CI threat. The two general categories of CI measures are active and passive.

Active CI measures are those measures that are designed to neutralize or eliminate the foreign intelligence effort and adversary sabotage, subversion, and terrorism capabilities. Counterreconnaissance operations and deception activities are examples of active measures that are routinely employed by all units. Complex active CI measures such as counterespionage operations, counterterrorism operations, screening and interrogations, and CI force protection source operations are conducted only by CI personnel or other specialized organizations following the direction of the joint force and/or MAGTF commanders. Passive CI measures are designed to conceal and deny information to foreign intelligence personnel and protect friendly personnel and installations from sabotage, subversion, and terrorism. Camouflage, security of classified material, emission control, information systems security, noise and light discipline, and physical access control are examples of passive CI measures that are employed extensively by all units. The CI process is summarized in figure 3-14.

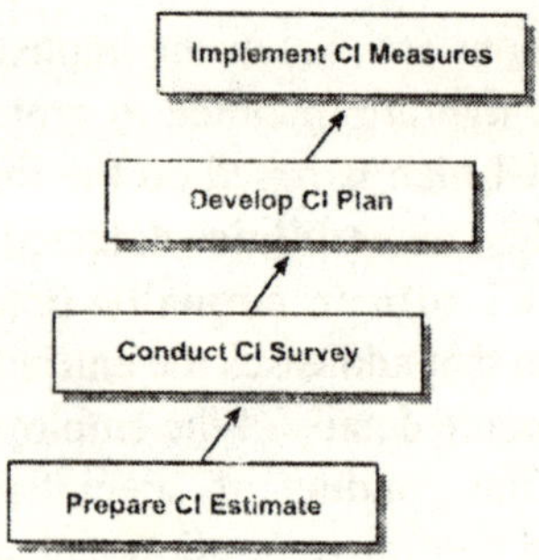

Figure 3-14. *The Counterintelligence Process.*

Chapter - 4

Concept of MAGTF Intelligence Support

Marine intelligence operations are conducted primarily to facilitate the planning and execution of MAGTF operations through the development of tactical intelligence. The concept of MAGTF intelligence support ensures that the required intelligence is available to commanders at all levels throughout the force in time to influence their decisionmaking process. Key elements of this concept follow:

• Fully manned and capable organic intelligence sections down to manoeuvre battalion/squadron level.

• Directing the intelligence effort and maintenance of a robust collection, production, and dissemination capability at the MAGTF level.

• Employing specialized intelligence units to provide dedicated collection, processing, exploitation, and production of all-source intelligence.

• Creating key intelligence nodes at any level to concentrate intelligence support at critical times and locations. (These nodes are created through task organization, split-basing, and the use of intelligence direct support teams [DSTs].) An intelligence DST provides an enhanced intelligence capability to a supported intelligence section. A DST consists of one officer and several enlisted intelligence specialists. DSTs are organic to the MEF and each MSC G-2 sections.

• Full use of the intelligence support available from national, theater, joint, other Service component, and multinational forces to enhance MAGTF intelligence capabilities.

• Augmentation from global sourcing (noncommitted operating forces, the supporting establishment, and the Reserves) to enhance intelligence support to the MAGTF.

This intelligence support concept provides organic intelligence sections to commanders at all levels. These sections develop intelligence to satisfy their units' unique requirements. This intelligence supports their commander's tactical decisionmaking process and generates tailored intelligence products to facilitate mission execution.

Unit intelligence sections are supported by a primary MAGTF intelligence node that can perform all types of intelligence operations. The MAGTF G-2, through its combat intelligence center (CIC), provides centralized direction for the collection, production, and dissemination efforts of organic and supporting intelligence assets and ensures that these efforts remain focused on satisfying the PIRs that are essentialto mission success. At the MEF CE level, the intelligence operations center (IOC) is the primary MAGTF intelligence node. Concentration of specialized intelligence capabilities in the radio battalion, the intelligence battalion, and the force reconnaissance company under this centralized direction facilitates unity of effort, effective employment of limited assets, and the collection and production of all-source intelligence.

The concept of intelligence support acknowledges the need to focus intelligence efforts in support of particular MAGTF elements during different phases of an operation. The MAGTF intelligence structure has the flexibility to provide such focused support through task organization. Enhanced support can be provided employing DSTs and integrating MAGTF intelligence assets.

Recognizing that organic intelligence capabilities may be limited in particular environments, the MAGTF can draw on the full range of national, theater, joint, other Service, allied, and multinational intelligence assets. When available, these capabilities will be fully integrated into MAGTF intelligence operations. If a separate Marine component headquarters is established, it will support the MAGTF by performing those intelligence functions not directly related to warfighting, to include the following:

- Conducting detailed operational-level intelligence planning.
- Providing Marine intelligence liaison to joint task force (JTF) and other component intelligence elements.
- Monitoring the status of MAGTF intelligence collection and production requests for supporting and external support requirements.
- Planning the development and monitoring the adequacy of the JTF/MAGTF's intelligence architectures and the flow of intelligence to the MAGTF.
- Supporting Marine participation in intelligence support to the joint targeting process.

If a separate Marine component headquarters is not established, then the MAGTF CE's CIC will perform these functions. MSCs and other MAGTF elements will be able to access these external capabilities through the MAGTF intelligence architecture to pull available intelligence products on demand. Specialized intelligence units; e.g., the radio battalion or intelligence battalion, will have connectivity with appropriate external agencies to coordinate tasking or support.

Any MAGTF that is committed to an operation can be supported by intelligence assets of nondeployed MAGTFs, the supporting establishment or the Reserves. This support could consist of augmentation to fill shortfalls in manpower, equipment or specialized capabilities and assistance in developing intelligence in response to a Serviceunique requirement. Flexibility to draw on assets from across the Marine Corps provides the ability to tailor and enhance particular intelligence capabilities based on the requirements of the committed MAGTF commander.

Role of the Organic Intelligence Section

Most commands from the battalion/squadron level and above in the operating forces have an organic intelligence section. The unit intelligence officer and section occupy the central role in the concept of MAGTF intelligence support. They focus the intelligence effort to develop, disseminate, and ensure effective use of intelligence in support of tactical operations. Intelligence drives operations and remains responsive to mission requirements through close and direct contact with the commander, key staff officers, and subordinate unit leaders.

The Unit Intelligence Officer

The commander directs the intelligence effort. The intelligence officer manages this effort for the commander, acting as the principal advisor on intelligence and implementing activities that carry out the commander's intelligence responsibilities. The intelligence officer is a full participant in the commander's decisionmaking process, ensuring that intelligence is effectively used throughout the command during all phases *of mission planning and execution.* Key responsibilities follow:

- Facilitate understanding and use of intelligence in the planning and execution of operations.
- Support situation development and the commander's estimate of the situation by identifying enemy capabilities, strengths, and critical vulnerabilities and opportunities and limitations presented by the environment.
- Assist the commander in developing PIRs.
- Ensure that the command's IRs are received, understood, and acted on by organic and supporting intelligence assets.
- Develop and disseminate all-source intelligence products that are tailored to the unit's mission and concept of operations.
- Monitor the effective flow of intelligence throughout the command.
- Provide BDA data and analysis to assist the combat assessment process.

The Unit Intelligence Section

The unit intelligence section supports the commander, the intelligence officer, and the entire command through the production and dissemination of mission-oriented intelligence products. Primary functions follow:

- Conduct IPB analysis for the unit's AO and interest.
- Develop and maintain a comprehensive intelligence estimate.

- Tailor intelligence produced at all levels to meet specific unit requirements.
- Form collection plans and support requests to satisfy unit PIRs and IRs.
- Maintain an accurate image of the battlespace and enemy situation.
- Prepare target analysis and target intelligence products.
- Recommend CI and force protection measures.
- Provide linkage to supporting intelligence assets.

Each organic intelligence section performs all six intelligence functions described in chapter 1. However, the priority and level of effort applied to the different functions will vary with the type of unit, level of command, and assigned mission. For example, an infantry battalion S-2 section will normally focus on support of the commander's estimate and situation development, while the S-2 of a combat service support (CSS) unit may concentrate on support of force protection, and the intelligence section of a fixed-wing Marine aircraft group usually places priority on support of targeting and combat assessment (particularly BDA).

Required Capabilities

To carry out these responsibilities, organic intelligence sections must have the following capabilities:

- Sufficient manning to carry out assigned responsibilities.
- Training in all aspects of tactical intelligence development, emphasizing the production of tailored, all-source, mission-specific intelligence products.
- Organic collection, processing, production, and dissemination assets appropriate to its mission and level of command.
- Connectivity to other MAGTF intelligence assets to provide a common picture of the battlespace, receive warning and other critical intelligence, and achieve access for "pulling" pertinent intelligence in response to unit requirements.

- Formation as a base for developing a larger intelligence support node, task-organized to provide expanded intelligence capabilities during particular phases of an operation.

The MAGTF Intelligence Section

The MAGTF intelligence section resident in the MAGTF CE is the focal point for intelligence operations and development in the MAGTF.

MAGTF Intelligence Officer

The MAGTF G-2/S-2, supported by the CIC and its subordinate sections, provides centralized direction for the MAGTF's comprehensive intelligence effort. The G-2/S-2 serves as the intelligence officer for the MAGTF commander. The CIC serves as the primary intelligence node for the entire MAGTF. As such, the CIC must remain responsive to the requirements of all MAGTF elements. The MAGTF intelligence section performs the following tasks:

- Provides centralized direction for MAGTF intelligence operations.
- Plans and implements a concept for intelligence support based on the mission, concept of operations, and commander's intent.
- Consolidates, validates, and prioritizes IRs of the MAGTF.
- Recommends MAGTF PIRs to the MAGTF commander.
- Maintains a consolidated, all-source production center in the MAGTF all-source fusion center (AFC).
- Plans, develops, and directs the MAGTF collection, production, and dissemination plans and operations.
- Directs the employment of MAGTF organic collection assets through the surveillance and reconnaissance cell (SARC) and the operations control and analysis center (OCAC).
- Submits consolidated requests for external intelligence support through the Marine component headquarters to appropriate agencies.

- Links the MAGTF to national, theater, joint, other Service, and multinational intelligence assets and operations.
- Prepares a comprehensive CI plan with recommended force protection measures.
- Supervises the execution of appropriate active and passive CI measures, CI functions, and CI services.

In addition to the responsibilities of all MAGTF intelligence officers, the MEF assistant chief of staff (AC/S) G-2 exercises staff cognizance over several special staff officers and their intelligence units/organizations.

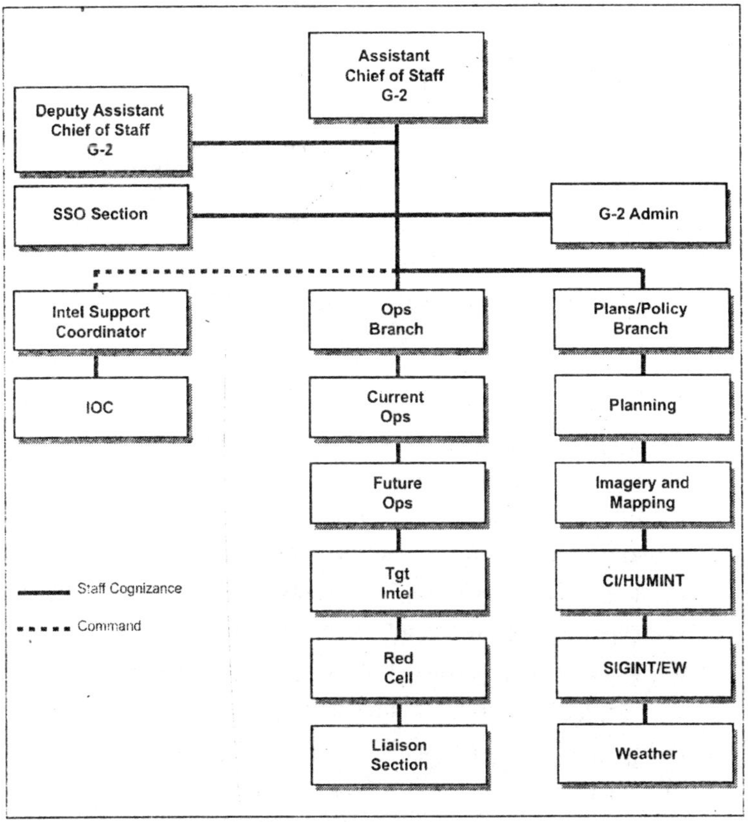

Figure 4-1. *Special Staff Officers and Relationships under the Staff Cognizance of the MEF G-2.*

The AC/S G-2 has staff responsibility for intelligence and intelligence operations. The commander relies on the intelligence officer to provide information on weather, terrain, and enemy capabilities, status, and intentions. Through the intelligence OPLAN and supporting intelligence, CI, and reconnaissance and surveillance (R&S) plans, the G-2 validates and plans information requirements; coordinates intelligence priorities, integrates collection, production, and dissemination activities; allocates resources; assigns specific intelligence and reconnaissance missions to subordinate elements; and supervises the overall intelligence, CI, and reconnaissance efforts. Specific responsibilities follow:

- Develop and answer outstanding MEF and subordinate units' priority information requirements and information requirements by planning, directing, integrating, and supervising organic multidiscipline MEF and supporting intelligence operations.
- Prepare appropriate intelligence, CI, and reconnaissance plans and orders for the MEF and review and coordinate the all-source intelligence CI and reconnaissance plans of JTFs, theaters, and other organizations.
- Submit and coordinate all-source collection, production, and dissemination requirements beyond the capability of the MEF to satisfy to higher headquarters for JTF, theater or national intelligence support.
- Ensure intelligence information is rapidly processed, analyzed, and incorporated where appropriate in all-source intelligence products, and rapidly disseminated to all MEF and external units requiring these.
- Evaluate JTF, theater, and national all-source intelligence support and adjusting stated IRs, if necessary.
- Identify and correct deficiencies in intelligence, CI, and reconnaissance personnel and equipment resources.
- Incorporate intelligence in training exercises to improve MEF individual, collective, and unit readiness.
- Facilitate understanding and use of intelligence in support of the planning and execution of MEF operations.

Special Staff Officers under the Staff

Cognizance of G-2 Officer

G-2 Operations Officer

The G-2 operations officer has primary responsibility for intelligence support to the commanding officer and the remainder of the CE in support of current and future operations. Specific responsibilities include the following:

- Coordinate and provide intelligence support to the commander, the G-3 operations section, and the rest of the commander's battle staff.
- Serve as the G-2 representative to the MEF CE crisis action team.
- Coordinate, provide, and supervise intelligence support to the MEF CE current operations center, future operations center, and force fires.
- Plan, direct, and supervise the Red Cell.
- Provide recommendations on PIR and IR validation, prioritization, and taskings to the AC/S G-2 and the intelligence support coordinator (ISC). The intelligence battalion commander is dual-hatted as the ISC.
- Coordinate and supervise the transition of intelligence planning and operations from G-2 plans to G-2 future operations, and from G-2 future operations to G-2 current operations, to effectively support the MEF's "single battle" transition process.
- Plan, direct, and supervise MEF liaison teams to external commands; e.g., the JTF and joint functional components headquarters, and intelligence organizations.
- Coordinate with the ISC and MEF MSCs' G-2 operations officers to ensure unity of effort of MEF intelligence operations.
- Provide intelligence input and other support to MEF warning and fragmentary orders and to operations related reporting; e.g., periodic situation reports.

- Coordinate intelligence training for the MEF G-2 section and providing G-2 oversight for and integration of the entire MEF intelligence training program.
- Perform other intelligence support and tasks as directed by the AC/S G-2.

G-2 Plans Officer

The G-2 plans officer has primary responsibility for intelligence support to the future plans cell. Specific responsibilities follow:

- Plan the MEF concept of intelligence operations for approval by the AC/S G-2 and subsequent implementation by the integrated staff cell based upon the mission, threat, commander's intent, guidance, and concept of operations.
- Lead, coordinate, and provide intelligence support to MEF G-5 future plans section.
- Plan and coordinate intelligence support requirements for and the deployment of intelligence elements and resources into the AO.
- Provide recommendations on PIR and IR validation, prioritization, and taskings to the AC/S G-2 and the ISC.
- Coordinate, in conjunction with the ISC, G-2 development of Annex B (Intelligence) and Annex M (Geospatial Information and Services) to MEF OPLANs.
- Keep the G-2 section, other CE staff sections, intelligence liaison personnel, augmentees, and others apprised of MEF intelligence planning actions and requirements.
- Identify requirements and provide recommendations to the G-2 operations officer for MEF intelligence liaison teams to external commands; e.g., the JTF or other components' headquarters and intelligence agencies.
- Coordinate and develop policies for MEF intelligence, CI, and reconnaissance operations.
- Plan, direct, and supervise the MEF G-2's imagery and mapping, CI/HUMINT, SIGINT, and weather sections.
- Perform other intelligence support and tasks as directed by the AC/S G-2.

Intelligence Battalion Commander/Intelligence Support Coordinator

The intelligence battalion commander is responsible for planning, directing, collecting, processing, producing and disseminating intelligence, and providing CI support to the MEF, MEF MSCs, subordinate MAGTFs, and other commands as directed.

Garrison: In garrison the principal task of the intelligence battalion commander is to organize, train, and equip detachments that support MAGTFs or other designated commands to execute integrated collection, intelligence analysis, production, and dissemination of intelligence products.

During Operations: During operations the intelligence battalion commander is dual-hatted as the ISC, serving as such under the direct staff cognizance of the MEF AC/S G-2. The intelligence battalion's S-3 section, along with the operations center element of the MEF G-2, form the core of the ISC support effort, with planning, direction, and C2 conducted within the IOC's support cell. As the ISC, he is responsible to the MEF AC/S G-2 for the overall planning and execution of MEF all-source intelligence operations. Specific responsibilities of the ISC during actual operations follow:

- Implement the concept of intelligence operations developed by the G-2 plans officer and approved by the AC/S G-2.
- Establish and supervise operation of the MEF IOC, which includes the support cell, the SARC, and the production and analysis (P&A) cell. Generally the IOC will be collocated with the MEF CE's main CP.
- Develop, consolidate, validate, and prioritize recommended PIRs and IRs to support MAGTF planning and operations. The ISC is tasked to perform PIR and IR validation and prioritization *only* during operations when the IOC is activated. During routine peacetime operations, the PIR/IR validation and prioritization tasks are the responsibility of the MEF CE's G-2 operations officer.
- Plan, develop, integrate, and coordinate MEF intelligence collection, production, and dissemination plans, to include

the effective organic and external integration and employment and staff cognizance of MEF SIGINT, CI, HUMINT, geographic intelligence, IMINT, ground remote sensors, ground reconnaissance, and tactical air reconnaissance intelligence collections, production, and dissemination operations.

- Develop, in conjunction with the G-2 plans officer and G-2 operations officer, and complete Annex B (Intelligence) and Annex M (Geospatial Information and Services) to MEF operation orders (OPORDs).
- Plan, develop, integrate, and coordinate intelligence and CI support to the commander's estimate, situation development, I&W, force protection, targeting, and combat assessment.
- Manage and fuse the threat (or *red*) common operational picture (COP)/common tactical picture (CTP) inputs from subordinate units and external commands and intelligence agencies into the MEF CE's threat COP/CTP.
- Provide intelligence support to the MEF CE G-2 section and the MSCs.
- Prepare the intelligence and CI estimates to support G-2 plans.
- Plan, develop, and coordinate intelligence CIS architecture, to include its integration with and support of MEF IMINT and other intelligence and reconnaissance requirements.
- Coordinate and integrate all-source intelligence operations with other Service components, JTF joint intelligence support element (JISE), theater joint intelligence center (JIC) or joint analysis center, and national intelligence agencies and operations to include all aspects of intelligence reach back support.
- Assist with the evaluation and improvement of MEF all-source intelligence, CI, and reconnaissance operations.
- Perform other intelligence support and tasks as directed by the AC/S G-2.

Intelligence Support Coordinator

- Plan and execute intelligence operations to support all MEF IRs.
- Establish and direct the IOC (P&A cell, SARC, and support cell).
- IR management (collection, production and dissemination) validation, prioritization, and tasking per AC/S G-2 direction.
- Intelligence operations command of intelligence battalion and staff cognizance over SIGINT, CI, HUMINT, MASINT, IMINT, and air/ground reconnaissance (or designated G-2 elements).

G-2 Operations Officer

- Intelligence support to MEF CE battlestaff and current operations center agencies.
- Coordination and support to higher and adjacent headquarters and agencies.
- Recommends IR validation, prioritization, and tasking to AC/S G-2.
- Establish and direct intelligence elements and support to the current operations center, future operations center, target intelligence section, force fires, Red Cell, and MEF intelligence liaison teams.

G-2 Plans Officer

- Intelligence support to the G-5 future planning team for future planning IRs.
- Recommend IR validation, prioritization, and tasking to AC/S G-2.
- Establish and direct the G-2 future planning intelligence element.

• G-2 section's imagery & mapping, CI/HUMINT, SIGINT, and weather sections (less that under the staff cognizance of the ISC).

Figure 4-2. *AC/S G-2's Principal Subordinate Staff Officers and their Responsibilities.*

Figure 4-2 is a summary of the principal responsibilities of the AC/S G-2's three principal subordinate staff officers.

Collection Management/Dissemination Officer: The collection management/dissemination officer (CMDO) is sourced from the intelligence battalion's S-3 section and is a key subordinate to the intelligence battalion commander/ISC during operations. The CMDO is responsible for formulating detailed intelligence collection requirements and intelligence dissemination requirements and tasking and coordinating internal and external operations to satisfy these. The CMDO receives validated PIRs and IRs and direction from the ISC, and then plans and manages the best methods to employ organic and supporting collection and dissemination resources through the intelligence collection and dissemination plans (tabs to Appendix 16, *Intelligence Operations Plan*, to Annex B.) The CMDO is also responsible for validating and forwarding national and theater intelligence collection requests from the MEF and MSCs typically using appropriate intelligence tools and TTP. He also is responsible for coordinating intelligence CIS requirements and maintaining awareness of available CIS connectivity throughout the MAGTF and with key external organizations.

During operations the CMDO works within the support cell. In coordination with the P&A cell officer in charge (OIC), the SARC OIC, G-2 operations officer, intelligence/reconnaissance commanding officers/OICs, and the MEF G-6, the CMDO is responsible to the ISC for the following tasks:

- Determine and coordinate the collection effort of PIRs/IRs that may be collected via intelligence, CI, and reconnaissance resources.
- Determine PIRs/IRs and prepare requests for intelligence that are beyond organic capabilities and prepare submissions to higher headquarters and external agencies for support.
- Recommend dissemination priorities, development of intelligence reporting criteria, and advise on and selecting dissemination means.
- Develop and coordinate all-source intelligence collection plans, coordinate and integrate these with MEF, other

components, JTF, theater, and national intelligence production operations.

- Develop and coordinate all-source intelligence dissemination plans and supporting architectures for voice and data networked communications, and coordinate and integrate these with MEF, other components, JTF, theater, and national intelligence CIS and dissemination operations.
- Monitor the flow of intelligence throughout the MEF and ensure that it is delivered to intended recipients in a timely fashion and satisfactorily meet their needs.
- Evaluate the effectiveness of MEF and supporting intelligence collection and dissemination operations.

SARC OIC

The SARC OIC is also an immediate subordinate of the ISC and is responsible for supervising the execution of the integrated organic, attached, and direct support intelligence collection and reconnaissance operations. The SARC OIC is responsible to the ISC for accomplishing the following specific responsibilities:

- Coordinate, monitor, and maintain the status of all ongoing intelligence, CI, and reconnaissance collection operations. This includes—
  - (a) Missions, tasked intelligence collection requirements, and reporting criteria for all collection missions.
  - (b) Locations and times for all pertinent fire support control measures.
  - (c) Primary and alternate CIS plans for routine and time-sensitive requirements for intelligence users (collectors, the SARC, and key MEF, CE, and MSC C2 nodes) to support ongoing C2 of collection operations and dissemination of acquired data and intelligence via the most expeditious means.
- Conduct detailed intelligence collection planning and coordination with the MSCs and intelligence, CI, and reconnaissance organizations' planners, with emphasis on ensuring understanding of the collection plan and specified intelligence reporting criteria.

- Ensure other MAGTF C2 nodes; e.g., the current operations center or force fires are apprised of ongoing intelligence, CI, and reconnaissance operations.
- Receive routine and time-sensitive intelligence reports from deployed collection elements; cross-cueing among intelligence collectors, as appropriate; and the rapid dissemination of intelligence reports to MAGTF C2 nodes and others in accordance with standing PIRs/IRs, intelligence reporting criteria and dissemination plan, and the current tactical situation.

P&A Cell OIC

The P&A cell OIC is the third principal subordinate to the ISC, with primary responsibility for managing and supervising the MEF's all-source intelligence processing and production efforts. Key responsibilities follow:

- Plan, direct, and manage operations of the AFP (to include the fusion, order of battle, IPB, and target intelligence/ battle damage assessment teams), the topographic platoon, the IIP, the DSTs, and other P&A elements as directed.
- Coordinate and integrate P&A cell operations, estimates, and products with the MEF G-2 section's G-2 operations branch and its Red Cell operations and estimates.
- Maintain all-source automated intelligence databases, files, workbooks, country studies, and other intelligence studies.
- Plan and maintain imagery, mapping, and topographic resources and other intelligence references.
- Administer, integrate, operate, and maintain intelligence processing and production systems, unclassified general service and senstitive compartmented information systems; e.g., the intelligence analysis system or the image product library.
- Analyze and fuse intelligence and other information into tailored all-source intelligence products to satisfy all supported commanders' stated or anticipated PIRs and IRs.

- Develop and maintain current and future intelligence situational, threat, and environmental assessments and target intelligence based upon all-source analysis, interpretation, and integration.

Manage and fuse the threat COP/CTP inputs from subordinate units and external commands and intelligence agencies into the MEF CE's threat COP/CTP.

MAGTF Intelligence Units

The limited number of specialized intelligence assets, coupled with the requirement to integrate and focus intelligence operations on the satisfaction of the command's PIRs, creates the need for centralized management. Intelligence units whose capabilities support the entire MAGTF are employed in general support of the MAGTF with staff cognizance exercised through the G-2/S-2. Certain intelligence units are capable of performing operational tasks in addition to their primary intelligence functions. For example, a force reconnaissance team may carry out a laser target designation mission or a UAV may be used to assist in maneuver control. Likewise, radio battalion may support manoeuvre and fires through electronic attack operations. The MAGTF G-2/S-2 provides centralized direction for these assets and facilitates unity of effort, the production of all-source intelligence, and the effective use of limited resources in support of the requirements of the entire force. Direction is provided primarily through MAGTF-level intelligence C2 agencies; e.g., the SARC and the OCAC. Subordinate elements of the MAGTF retain organic intelligence assets and OPCON appropriate to their mission and level of command; e.g., division ground reconnaissance units remain under the OPCON of the division commander.

Organization of MAGTF-Level

Intelligence Units

Radio Battalion

The radio battalion provides ground-based SIGINT, electronic warfare (EW), communications security monitoring, and special intelligence communications capability to support MAGTF operations. In addition to directing the employment of its subordinate elements, the radio battalion is the focal point for MAGTF ground-based SIGINT operations. It plans and coordinates these activities through the OCAC.

Intelligence Battalion

The intelligence battalion plans, directs, collects, produces, and disseminates intelligence and provides CI support to the MEF, MSCs, subordinate MAGTFs and other commands as directed. This support is usually provided by a task-organized detachment sent to the supported command. Within the intelligence battalion is a headquarters company, a P&A company, and a CI/HUMINT company.

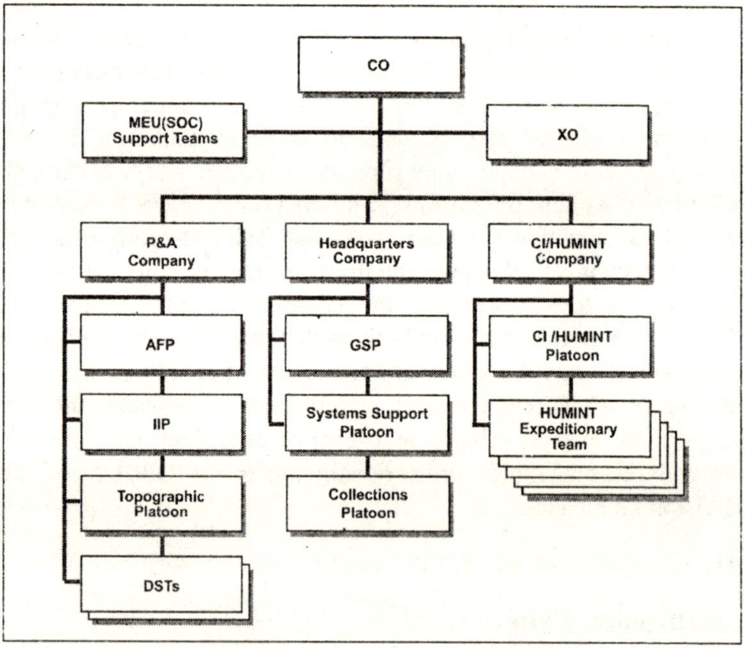

Figure 4-3. *Intelligence Battalion.*

Headquarters Company

The headquarters company consists of a systems support platoon, collections platoon, and the GSP. The systems support platoon maintains the intelligence systems within the battalion in garrison and in the field should the battalion deploy. The collections platoon manages intelligence requirements for the battalion. The GSP isresponsible for planning, controlling, and managing the employment of unattended ground remote sensor equipment in support of MAGTF operations or other commands as directed.

P&A Company

The P&A company consists of an AFP, a topographic platoon, and an IIP. The AFP provides fused intelligence to the supported MAGTF and assists MSC intelligence sections in providing situational awareness to their commanders and staff. The topographic platoon provides geographic intelligence products and services, geodetic and topographic surveys, and hydrographic analysis. The IIP provides imagery analysis support and dissemination to the MAGTF and other commands as directed.

CI/HUMINT Company

The CI/HUMINT company provides CI and HUMINT support to MAGTF operations. This support encompasses the full range of tactical CI and HUMINT operations, including screening operations, interrogation/debriefing of enemy prisoners of war and persons of intelligence interest, conduct of CI force protection source operations, conduct of CI surveys and investigations, preparation of CI estimates and plans, translation of documents, and limited exploitation of captured material. In addition, the CI/HUMINT company maintains a technical surveillance countermeasures team with equipment. CI/HUMINT Marines deploy as a task-organized HUMINT exploitation team (HET) in direct support of MAGTF's and subordinate elements.

Force Reconnaissance Company

The force reconnaissance company conducts preassault and deep postassault R&S in support of MAGTF operations. The company uses specialized insertion, patrolling, reporting, and extraction techniques to carry out amphibious and deep R&S tasks in support of the MAGTF. The company can perform a variety of other operational tasks. When a conflict exists between the requirements for R&S and other missions, the MAGTF commander determines the priority of tasking for the company based on recommendations from the G-2/S-2 and G-3/S-3.

Marine Unmanned Aerial Vehicle Squadron (VMU)

VMUs provide day/night, real-time imagery reconnaissance, surveillance, and target acquisition in support of the MAGTF. The unique capabilities of the UAV can also be used to support target engagement, assisting in the control of fires/supporting arms and maneuver. Squadrons are under the administrative control of the Marine aircraft wing (MAW). However, because of the limited number of assets and the critical capabilities they provide to the entire force, the MAGTF commander retains OPCON of the VMUs.

Employment of MAGTF Intelligence Units

MAGTF intelligence units are employed to meet the requirements of the entire force. The MAGTF G-2/S-2 develops a concept of intelligence support, which employs these units on the basis of the MAGTF mission, PIRs, concept of operations, and commander's intent. This concept must integrate intelligence activities with operations to provide key intelligence to commanders to enable rapid and effective decisionmaking. Based on the results of IPB analysis and the concept of operations, assets are positioned to satisfy PIRs, expose enemy vulnerabilities, monitor key locations, detect and assist in the engagement of targets, and identify opportunities as they arise in the battlespace.

Intelligence units are employed in either general or direct support. Under general support, units are tasked by the MAGTF commander through his G-2/S-2 to satisfy the requirements of the entire force. Because of the limited number of specialized intelligence assets and their ability to develop intelligence that is relevant to current and future operations in all areas of the battlespace (deep, close, and rear), general support is the preferred support relationship. Under direct support, the requirements of a supported commander are given priority. Direct support is used to focus intelligence support for particular phases of an operation or to create enhanced intelligence nodes in support of MAGTF subordinate elements. When MAGTFs smaller than a full MEF are deployed, they will normally be supported by attached, task-organized detachments from the intelligence battalion, the force reconnaissance company, and the radio battalion.

Focused Intelligence Support

Intelligence must be integrated with the mission, commander's intent, and concept of operations and should normally be weighted to support the main effort. The MAGTF intelligence structure has the flexibility to tailor its capabilities to meet the requirements of various types of expeditionary operations and to adapt to changing operational needs during the execution. For each operation, the MAGTF G-2/S-2 will assess the IRs and develop a concept of intelligence support that positions assets where they can best satisfy those requirements. Intelligence nodes will be used to focus support within the MAGTF. Split-basing will be used to build intelligence nodes within and outside the AO to deliver comprehensive and reliable intelligence support while reducing the size of the deployed force. Intelligence units and DSTs are employed to tailor and enhance the capabilities of organic intelligence sections or to create task-organized intelligence nodes in response to specific requirements.

Intelligence Nodes

The MAGTF can create a series of intelligence nodes, thereby providing focused intelligence support to specific units or areas based on the tactical situation. In the concept of intelligence support, the MAGTF G-2/S-2, in conjunction with the MSC intelligence officers, task-organizes the MAGTF's intelligence units and uses intelligence DSTs to deliver the required intelligence capabilities at key points and times. Although these nodes normally support a specific unit, they can also be used in an area-support mode where an intelligence node is established to support all units operating in a particular sector of the battlespace. For example, during sustained operations ashore, an intelligence node could be built to support units operating in the MAGTF's rear area. Such a node could be built around a DST and specialists from the CI/HUMINT company and topographic platoon. This node might support the rear area operations center, CSSE units operating in the area or any security detachments located within the node's area of responsibility.

Split-basing

Intelligence nodes can also be used to tailor the footprint of the intelligence organization within and outside of a designated AO. Intelligence assets are positioned where they can best carry out their assigned functions. In many cases, it may not be necessary or desirable to forward deploy the entire MAGTF intelligence structure. The concept of operations, C2 support system, physical space limitations, and resource and/or logistical or other constraints may require the split-basing of intelligence assets.

Split-basing is the positioning of critical capabilities within the AO to support the deployed commander and forces, while maintaining indepth intelligence management, processing, exploitation, analysis, and production elements in rear areas, intermediate support bases, staging areas or garrison locations. Split-basing enables reach back capabilities and can enhance the intelligence effort by providing continued access to sophisticated, nondeployable intelligence capabilities and resources. At the same time, it reduces the footprint of the deployed force, diminishing risk from enemy action and decreasing the administrative and logistic support requirements.

Split-basing is especially useful—

- When operations are conducted in areas with minimal infrastructure and support.
- When there are limitations on the number of personnel who can be deployed within the operating area.
- During the deployment phase when it may not be possible to immediately move all required elements of the intelligence structure to the forward area.

However, the advantages of split-basing must be assessed against its costs, particularly its critical dependence on responsive and reliable communications support.

Task Organization of Intelligence

Support Units

Task organization of intelligence support units is one of the principal means for the MAGTF commander to shape the intelligence effort. The collection, exploitation, and unique production capabilities of specialized intelligence units significantly enhance the ability of supported G-2/S-2 sections to develop timely, mission-focused intelligence.

Intelligence battalion, force reconnaissance company, and radio battalion elements are task-organized to provide tailored intelligence capabilities. Specific capabilities provided are based on the threat, the supported unit's anticipated requirements (as determined through IPB), and the concept of operations. Elements from some or all of the intelligence battalion's subordinate companies are combined into intelligence battalion detachments. The CI/HUMINT company provides HETs. The radio battalion forms task-organized SIGINT support units (SSUs), which provide a mix of SIGINT and EW capabilities.

When MAGTFs smaller than a full MEF deploy, an intelligence battalion detachment, a HET, force reconnaissance platoons, and a radio battalion SSU will normally be attached to the MAGTF CE. In MEF operations, when the entire radio battalion, intelligence battalion, and force reconnaissance company are employed, detachments, HETs, SSUs, and platoons may be placed in direct support as required to provide tailored intelligence capabilities or to create an enhanced intelligence node in support of an MSC or other MAGTF element.

Intelligence DSTs

Intelligence DSTs are organic to the intelligence battalion and each of the division, MAW, and force service support group G-2 sections. Teams are made up of one officer and several enlisted personnel who have a mix of intelligence specialty skills. DSTs are used to provide an enhanced analytical and dissemination capability to a unit intelligence section and to link the intelligence structure to the supported units. As assigned by the G-2, they augment the supported unit's intelligence section to carry out the following tasks:

- Perform P&A in support of future operations.
- Tailor AFC and other external source intelligence products to the needs of the supported commander.

- Assist in the management of external intelligence support requirements.
- Facilitate dissemination of intelligence received from external sources.

The MEF and MSC G-2s use their DSTs to tailor and focus intelligence support to units designated as the main effort or to create enhanced intelligence nodes at key times and places in the battlespace.

Intelligence Coordination

Establishing and supervising operation of the MEF IOC, which includes the support cell, the SARC, and the P&A cell, requires a high degree of coordinationat all levels. Generally the IOC will be collocated with the MEF CE's main CP. See figure 4-4 for the basic IOC organization.

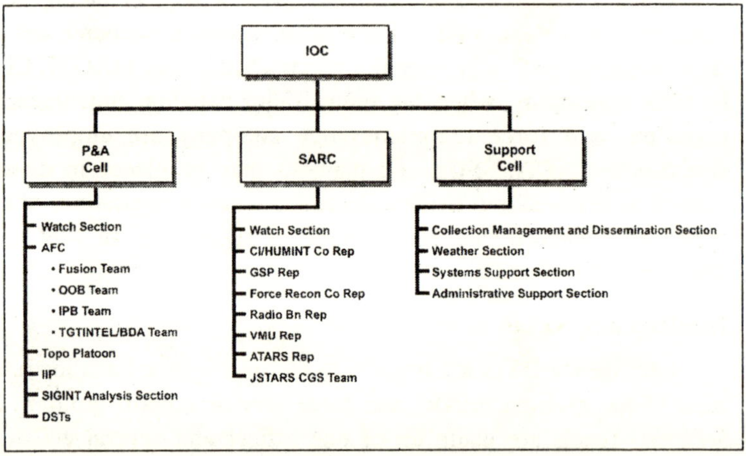

Figure 4-4. *Intelligence Operations Center.*

External Intelligence Support to the MAGTF

MARFOR Component Intelligence Section

Future military operations will normally be joint operations and may require establishing a MARFOR component headquarters. The Marine component is the level of command that deals directly with the JFC—the theater combatant commander or JTF commander—

for MARFORs assigned to combatant command or the JTF. The Marine component functions at the operational level of war to advise and assist the JFC in employing MARFORs while supporting the MAGTF. The Marine component commander coordinates operational actions with the JFC and the other component commanders so that the MAGTF commander can concentrate on warfighting.

Responsibilities

The Marine component intelligence section plays a crucial role in supporting the component commander and staff and in providing intelligence support to the MAGTF. The Marine component supports and enhances the planning and execution of MAGTF intelligence operations through close and continuous coordination with the JFC, joint force headquarters, and other component intelligence organizations. The Marine component G-2 section maintains situational awareness and provides a limited analytical capability to support the component future planning responsibility. It does not normally conduct collection operations or engage in detailed, formal intelligence production. It facilitates, but does not control, the flow of intelligence to the MAGTF. The component relieves the MAGTF commander of intelligence functions that are not directly related to warfighting.

Functions

The size of the Marine component G-2 section will vary with the size of the JTF and the scope of the operation. For major joint operations, the Marine component intelligence section provides the following functions:

- **Planning:** The intelligence section plans and coordinates component and MAGTF connectivity to national, theater, and JTF intelligence architectures. The Marine component develops the architecture to provide the MAGTF with timely, tailored national and theater intelligence. The component G-2 coordinates the provision of additional Service intelligence support (units, personnel, and equipment) to the MAGTF through the Service chain of command.

- **Collection management:** The intelligence section monitors the status of MAGTF collection requests for supporting and external collection resources. The MARFOR leverages joint and national collection resources in support of the MAGTF. It advocates Service component and MAGTF requirements in theater and JTF collection forums and recommends the allocation and tasking of national, JTF, and other component assets to meet MAGTF requirements.
- **P&A:** The intelligence section provides situational awareness to the component commander and staff and limited P&A to support the future planning responsibilities of the component headquarters. This function requires the establishment of a watch section and an analytical element that can tailor operational-level intelligence products to satisfy the needs of component planning cells. The component G-2 monitors the status of and coordinates support for MAGTF production requirements and requests for intelligence that are submitted to joint force or supporting intelligence agencies.
- **Dissemination:** The intelligence section monitors the adequacy of the intelligence architecture and the flow of intelligence to the MAGTF. Intelligence is disseminated directly to the appropriate MAGTF elements, not through the component headquarters unless specifically required. However, the MARFOR facilitates and accelerates the flow of critical intelligence to the MAGTF. The component intelligence section remains aware of current MAGTF requirements and ensures that intelligence that is developed or received by the theater or JTF that can satisfy those requirements is disseminated to the MAGTF.
- **Support of targeting:** The intelligence section supports Marine component participation in the joint targeting process, including representation at various joint target intelligence and/or targeting forums as required. Performing this function ensures that MAGTF target intelligence collection and production requirements as well as collection requirements for support of combat assessment/BDA are adequately supported.

Liaison

The intelligence section provides liaison elements and personnel augmentation to various JTF and other component intelligence organizations. Liaison elements may be provided to the following:

- JISE.
- Other Service or functional component intelligence sections.
- The regional SIGINT operations center.
- The joint force J-2 CI/HUMINT staff element.
- The HUMINT operations cell.
- Task force CI coordinating authority, other joint intelligence organizations such as the joint interrogation and debriefing center or the joint document exploitation center.
- The intelligence elements of various alliance or coalition partners.

Liaison teams or personnel augmentation may be sourced from the Marine component G-2 section, Service augmentation to the component G-2 section, the MAGTF, or some combination of the above.

National, Theater, Joint, and Other Service

Intelligence Support

Marine Corps intelligence assets are optimized for the production of tactical intelligence in support of MAGTF operations. National, theater, joint, and other Service intelligence assets provide unique capabilities that are not duplicated in the MAGTF intelligence support structure. (See figure 4-5.) The MAGTF has the ability to use external intelligence assets to enhance its organic capabilities, bringing the full range of these resources to bear on MAGTF requirements. The following are key external capabilities that support MAGTF operations:

- National- and theater-level intelligence analysis and production.
- Geospatial information and services (GI&S). GI&S describes the collection, production, and dissemination of

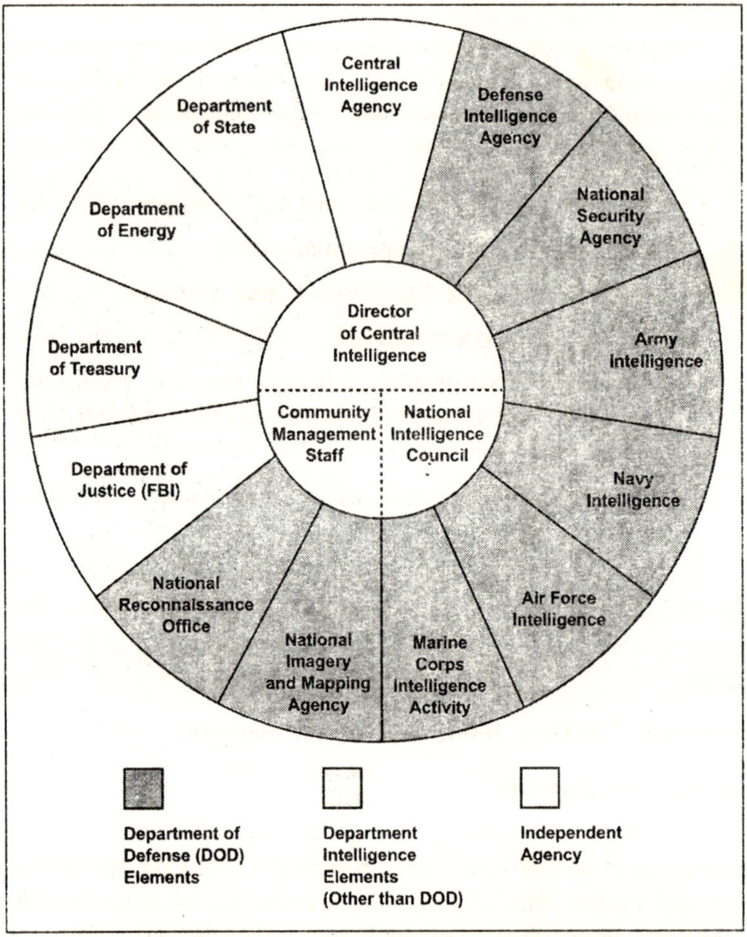

Figure 4-5. *The National Intelligence Community.*

information about the earth, and replaces the term mapping, charting, and geodesy.

- Analysis and production of target intelligence and target materials.
- National imagery collection and exploitation.
- SIGINT support from the National Security Agency and the US Cryptologic System.

- National- and theater-level CI and HUMINT collection.
- Liaison elements from national and theater intelligence agencies.

MAGTF Access to External Support: The Marine component headquarters or the MAGTF intelligence section will be the focal point for all external intelligence support to the MAGTF. In major joint operations, a Marine Service component headquarters will be established, and the component G-2 performs this function. When no Service component headquarters is established, the MAGTF acts in this role. Intelligence derived from external sources is used to build a common picture of the battlespace and is incorporated into other intelligence products that are provided to all MAGTF elements. MSCs and other subordinate units will be able to access external intelligence support resources through the MAGTF's intelligence architecture.

Required Capabilities

The following capabilities are required to fully use the resources of external intelligence support assets:

- Personnel trained and experienced in the capabilities, limitations, tasking, and employment procedures of external intelligence support assets.
- Sufficient, reliable CIS connectivity and interoperability with national, theater, and other Service intelligence C2 centers and architectures.
- The ability to receive, process, and disseminate information gathered by national and theater collection assets.
- Integrating Marine intelligence specialists into national, theater, and Service intelligence organizations to articulate Marine Corps capabilities and requirements and to optimize intelligence support to expeditionary forces.
- Establishing liaison between the MARFOR/MAGTF and supporting intelligence agencies through dedicated communications and the exchange of liaison officers.

Augmentation

Like all MAGTF components, intelligence support assets are flexible and respond to a variety of operational missions. They are configured for rapid deployment and can be tailored to meet the requirements of a particular operation. Although each MAGTF is furnished with a baseline intelligence capability to accomplish its anticipated mission, changes in the situation or mission tasking may require augmentation. When a MAGTF is committed to an operation, the intelligence assets of any remaining units in the operating forces can be called on to provide this augmentation. MAGTFs smaller than a MEF will normally be supported by their parent MEF; a fully deployed MEF can be augmented by the assets of any other MEF. Augmentation may consist of providing entire intelligence units, selected equipment or individual personnel with specialized skills. Support may also consist of providing intelligence products that cannot be developed by the deployed MAGTF or its supporting joint intelligence activity.

Supporting Establishment

Marine intelligence personnel and organizations of the supporting establishment enhance and sustain the intelligence activities of the operating forces.

Marine Corps Intelligence Activity

The Marine Corps maintains a Service-level intelligence capability in the Marine Corps Intelligence Activity (MCIA). MCIA focuses on crisis and predeployment support to expeditionary warfare. It complements the efforts of theater, other Service, and national intelligence organizations. It provides unique threat, technical, and geographic intelligence products that are tailored to Marine Corps operating forces preparing for deployment. It also coordinates Marine Corps Service collection, production, and dissemination requirements by acting as the Service collection, production, and dissemination manager. MCIA is collocated with the National Maritime Intelligence Center, Suitland, MD and at Marine Corps Base, Quantico, VA.

Marine Cryptologic Support Battalion

The Marine cryptologic support battalion provides Marine Corps participation in national and Department of the Navy cryptologic activities worldwide. These Marines perform tasks that are directly related to their military occupational specialty, contributing to the national, theater, and Department of the Navy SIGINT collection, production, and dissemination effort while gaining invaluable skill maintenance and enhancement opportunities. The battalion is collocated with the Naval Security Group, Fort Meade, MD and augments the operating forces with trained SIGINT personnel during crises and exercises.

Navy Marine Corps Intelligence Training Center

The Navy Marine Corps Intelligence Training Center (NMITC), Dam Neck, VA trains Navy and Marine Corps personnel in basic, intermediate, and advanced intelligence methods and applications. During contingency operations, NMITC supports the operating forces through the provision of intelligence training via mobile training teams and/or selective personnel augmentation.

Personnel Augmentation

The supporting establishment is also a source of experienced intelligence personnel who can be called on to fill contingency billets in the intelligence structure of a deploying or committed MAGTF.

Marine Corps Forces Reserve

The mission of Marine Corps Forces Reserve is to provide trained units and/or personnel to augment, reinforce or reconstitute active duty MARFORs during times of war or national emergency. Intelligence capabilities of the Marine Corps Reserve are complementary to those of the active component. This includes individual mobilization augmentee and individual ready reserve personnel and selected Marine Corps Reserve units (including two force reconnaissance companies), a GSP, an imagery interpretation unit, and several interrogator-translator and CI teams, which provide increased depth to limited active component capabilities.

Individual mobilization augmentee members of the Marine Corps Reserve Intelligence Programme and the Marine Corps Reserve Cryptologic Program routinely support the training and operational activities of the active component.

Chapter - 5

Operational Manoeuvre from the Sea

OMFTS is the manoeuvre of naval forces at the operational level that projects sea-based power ashore to deal a decisive blow. OMFTS is a bold bid for victory that aims to exploit a significant enemy weakness. It embodies the application of the principles of manoeuvre warfare to a maritime campaign. Success in OMFTS depends on the ability to seize fleeting opportunities and quickly take advantage of exposed enemy vulnerabilities.

OMFTS relies on intelligence to drive planning, option selection, and manoeuvre execution. To support OMFTS, intelligence operations must be conducted across the strategic, operational, and tactical levels of war. Starting with strategic considerations and working down to tactical dispositions, intelligence uncovers the threat's COG, strengths, and weaknesses, thereby exposing critical vulnerabilities to be exploited by naval forces operating from the sea. Intelligence also assesses the potential for manoeuvre offered by the battlespace, including identifying entry points where the force can establish itself ashore. The term entry point encompasses beaches, boat landing sites, HLZs, and drop zones that can establish elements of the force ashore. Intelligence also provides the foundation for effective force protection and IO efforts. These efforts help surprise, preempt, disrupt, and disorient the enemy during OMFTS execution.

Required Intelligence Capabilitites

- Perform IPB and situation development covering a broad manoeuvre space.

- Analyze threat forces to determine COG and critical vulnerabilities.
- Conduct detailed terrain and hydrographic analysis to identify suitable entry points.
- Ensure connectivity and interoperability with national, theater, and joint forces' intelligence assets, which provide intelligence support before the arrival of naval forces in the objective area.
- Provide stand-off collection assets that can satisfy force requirements from over-the-horizon.
- Provide organic imagery, SIGINT, HUMINT, CI, remote sensor, GI&S, and ground and aerial reconnaissance assets that can satisfy MAGTF tactical collection requirements as the force transitions ashore.
- Provide responsive processing, exploitation, and production capabilities that can rapidly develop the critical intelligence required to support timely decisionmaking.
- Provide dissemination systems that link widely dispersed forces afloat and ashore.
- Provide flexible intelligence units and organizations that can rapidly transition ashore with minimal degradation of support.
- Provide in-depth support to force protection and information operations activities.

Planning and Direction

There are a number of unique intelligence considerations for OMFTS. (See figure 5-1) During the planning phase, the MAGTF intelligence officer provides centralized direction for the intelligence efforts of the entire MAGTF. Navy and Marine intelligence assets operate together from an afloat amphibious force intelligence center, which is normally located on the amphibious force flagship. Initial requirements are broad in scope and are aimed at providing a general description of the battlespace and the threat. As planning progresses, requirements become increasingly focused on uncovering

Intelligence Cycle	*Key Considerations*
Planning and direction.	Centralized direction from ATFIC. Transitioning of key capabilities ashore.
Collection.	Initial dependence on national/theater capabilities. Employment of organic assets in advance force/preassault operations.
Processing, exploitation, and production.	Broad-based effort focusing on entry points and enemy vulnerabilities. Extensive support to CI and IO.
Dissemination.	Widely dispersed units afloat and ashore. Need for rapid intelligence flow to exploit fleeting opportunities.
Utilization.	COA selection shaped by intelligence. Choice of entry points, objectives, and targets driven by intelligence.

Figure 5-1. *Intelligence Considerations*

critical vulnerabilities and providing intelligence that is relevant to the COAs under consideration. The intelligence flow will be predominately from the top down—from national and theater activities—until organic naval intelligence capabilities can be brought to bear. A comprehensive, systematic management effort is required to ensure that the necessary support is requested and received. At the same time, Navy and Marine intelligence officers must also develop detailed plans for the positioning and employment of the organic intelligence assets to support the concept of operations.

Collection

Collection operations in the planning phase are conducted primarily by national and theater assets. These assets can collect information in denied areas without compromising operational security and/or perform their missions at significant stand-off distances. However, the small number of these systems and inherent limitations on their capabilities normally result in developing an incomplete intelligence picture. Advance force or preassault collection operations by naval assets will often be required to confirm and further develop the situation. An intensive intelligence effort must be provided in support of advance force or preassault operations; this intelligence support is required to select the proper targets for advance force or preassault collection operations, and ensure that these activities do not reveal the intent of the overall operation.

Processing, Exploitation, and Production

Initial production efforts are directed at providing an extensive description of the battlespace and threat. This description is required to focus the planning effort. Under the direction of senior Navy and Marine intelligence officers, the MAGTF, GCE, ACE, CSSE, Navy amphibious staff, and flagship intelligence sections engage in a cooperative effort to develop intelligence products that support the entire force. Individual intelligence sections will normally concentrate on their particular areas of expertise, thereby satisfying their units' requirements while contributing a broad-scope product to the general intelligence production effort. For example, the MAGTF G-2/AFC may focus on describing the battlespace and the enemy's C2, logistics, and reserves, while the GCE studies enemy ground forces, the ACE looks at the air and air defence threats, and the flagship intelligence department concentrates on the naval and coastal defence threat. From this effort, the ATFIC provides a comprehensive IPB analysis, an intelligence estimate, and supporting intelligence studies and products. As the planning phase continues, production efforts concentrate on identifying enemy vulnerabilities to be exploited and providing estimates and other intelligence products to support the specific COAs that are under consideration.

In the final stages of the OMFTS planning process, the production effort shifts to developing mission-specific intelligence products that focus on the selected COAs. These products include IPB graphics, beach and HLZ studies, and target/objective area studies. An extensive all-source intelligence effort is conducted to support deception, OPSEC, psychological operations (PSYOP), and EW planning in accordance with the MAGTF commander's overall IO strategy. During this stage, the production effort becomes increasingly decentralized as GCE, ACE, and CSSE intelligence sections focus on specific requirements of their units. The MAGTF intelligence section continues to provide products to support the entire force, with efforts concentrated on those MAGTF elements designated as the main effort.

Dissemination

Dissemination in OMFTS presents significant challenges. Naval forces can be widely dispersed and may not assemble until late in the planning phase, if at all. Advances in technology have improved the capability to disseminate information between forces afloat, but there continue to be limitations on the quantity and quality of intelligence that can be exchanged. In particular, dissemination systems will be taxed by the volume of intelligence products, especially critical graphic products that must be distributed during the planning phase. Intelligence officers at all levels, working in coordination with unit operations and CIS officers, must develop plans that provide for dissemination of key intelligence in a timely manner to all elements of the MAGTF. They must be particularly careful to include in these plans units located on ships that are not equipped with the latest C2 or intelligence systems.

Utilization

During the planning phase, intelligence is used to develop and select COAs and prepare detailed plans for implementing the selected COAs. After providing an initial orientation to the battlespace and the threat, the intelligence officer assists the commander and the staff in analyzing the enemy's strengths and weaknesses to identify COG and critical vulnerabilities that can be exploited. COAs are developed that take advantage of identified weaknesses to accomplish the assigned objective. The intelligence effort is refined on the basis of the COAs under consideration, providing answers to IRs generated during COA development. The intelligence developed through this interactive process aids the commander in selecting a favorable COA. Once the COA is chosen, intelligence shapes the concept of operations and supporting plans. Designation of objectives; selecting entry means, points, and times; and identifying targets are all based primarily on intelligence. Particular attention is given to steps that preserve surprise and that preempt, disrupt or disorient the enemy's response to our actions; e.g., force protection measures, and IO (including, but not limited to, physical destruction, military deception, OPSEC, PSYOP, and EW) plans.

Planning and Direction

The ATFIC will continue to act as the central node for the direction of the intelligence effort. As the operation unfolds, intelligence nodes can be established ashore to support units carrying out mission tasking. Depending on the nature and scope of the operation, most of the MAGTF intelligence structure can remain afloat or all of it may transition ashore. Movement of significant portions of the MAGTF intelligence structure ashore must be planned in detail to ensure a rapid transition with minimal degradation of support capability. If it is fully established ashore, the MAGTF intelligence section becomes the central node for intelligence direction. The ATFIC acts in a supporting capacity and continues to provide connectivity and services that cannot be readily established ashore. IRs that arise during execution are normally time sensitive. Intelligence direction must anticipate these requirements and establish a responsive collection, production, and dissemination structure to satisfy them. Designation of PIRs that are based on the results of IPB analysis, the commander's intent, and the concept of operations is critical. Using these factors to designate PIRs ensures that the intelligence effort remains focused on providing key intelligence to decisionmakers in a timely manner.

Collection

Collection operations transition from depending on national and theater capabilities to relying primarily on organic assets. Collection activities are integrated with the concept of operations. The objective is to develop the intelligence required to make key decisions regarding manoeuvre, targeting, and future plans. Collection assets are focused on key areas that are associated with the scheme of maneuver, location and development of critical targets, and combat assessment. Reports of units manoeuvring through the battlespace and/or in contact with the enemy are a significant source of information. This information must be transmitted to the appropriate intelligence section to help maintain situational awareness and refine the threat assessment. The MAGTF continues to employ national and theater- level collection support against targets located deep in the area of influence, throughout the area of interest, and against less time-sensitive requirements.

Processing, Exploitation, and Production

Rapid processing and production of intelligence are emphasized to support timely decisionmaking. OMFTS depends on decisive action and generating rapid operational tempo to break the enemy's cohesion and ability to resist. Intelligence sections must demonstrate the flexibility, agility, and responsiveness to quickly recognize enemy vulnerabilities and identify opportunities as they develop during the battle. To do this, intelligence sections at all levels must be aware of ongoing tactical activities and potential enemy reactions. They must be able to rapidly integrate all source intelligence information with sensor data and combat reporting to develop and maintain a coherent picture of enemy dispositions and an assessment of enemy intentions. They must be able to convey this picture and assessment (preferably in graphic form) to commanders in time to exploit identified opportunities. In addition to supporting the ongoing battle, intelligence sections must also be fully engaged in planning for future operations (continuing IPB analysis, delivering combat assessment inputs and BDA results, satisfying new IRs, and participating in the decisionmaking process).

Dissemination

Dissemination is an even greater challenge during OMFTS execution than during planning. Intelligence developed during the processing, exploitation, and production step must be rapidly disseminated to the units that are able to act on that intelligence. These forces may be widely dispersed afloat, airborne, and ashore while engaging in rapid manoeuvre and contact with the enemy. The dissemination system must be flexible and reliable and focus on the importance and quality of the intelligence distributed rather than on its volume. Dissemination plans must provide alarm channels for warning data and must ensure that pathways remain open for passing critical intelligence that directly affects PIRs or identified decision points. Measures that can help to reduce the volume of intelligence traffic follow:

- Limit routine reporting.
- Set filters to eliminate information that is not pertinent to the tactical situation.
- Establishing minimal reporting thresholds for the generation of intelligence reports.
- Providing alternate means for collection and other intelligence support requests.

Dissemination plans must permit two-way dissemination, providing a means for subordinate elements to pass along data, information or intelligence that they collect or develop that identifies new enemy vulnerabilities or enhances situation development for the entire force.

Utilization

Utilization of intelligence during the execution of OMFTS is rapid and decentralized. Intelligence identifies enemy vulnerabilities as the battle unfolds. Once developed, this intelligence is quickly disseminated to the MAGTF elements that can act on it, thereby enhancing the ability of individual units to exploit opportunities as they arise. Through integration with operations, assets are positioned to develop new intelligence as the concept of operations is carried out and the enemy responds. Timely collection, analysis, and dissemination of intelligence provides commanders with an accurate picture of the battlespace and the ability to recognize new opportunities as they arise. Commanders use this intelligence to select branches and sequels to the COA, attack targets, protect their own forces, assess the results of their actions, and plan future operations.

Chapter - 6

Sustained Operations Ashore

Sustained operations ashore require broad-based intelligence support that bridges the operational and tactical levels. Tactical plans are based on the results of operational-level intelligence assessments, which identify the enemy's COG and critical vulnerabilities throughout the theater of operations. MAGTF intelligence operations contribute to the operational-level assessments while translating the conclusions from these assessments into relevant tactical intelligence. Considerations for developing intelligence in support of sustained operations ashore are similar to those for OMFTS. Intelligence support during the execution of sustained operations ashore requires the same agility and responsiveness as in OMFTS, with the focus on providing critical intelligence to support timely decisionmaking. However, sustained operations ashore are normally conducted over a greater land area and with a larger force than in OMFTS, creating the requirement for a larger and more widely distributed intelligence support structure. The need for integration with theater, joint, multinational, and other Service intelligence assets is also greater.

Required Intelligence Capabilities

- Field and sustain intelligence structure to support MEF-level operations over extended periods.
- Execute all intelligence functions of a Service component headquarters, including full participation in theater or JTF intelligence activities.
- Ensure sufficient and reliable CIS systems connectivity and interoperability with theater, joint, and other Service intelligence assets participating in the operation.

- Conduct IPB and situation development in support of operational- and tactical-level planning.
- Provide organic imagery, SIGINT, CI, HUMINT, remote sensor, GI&S, and ground and aerial reconnaissance assets that can satisfy MAGTF tactical requirements.
- Provide processing, exploitation, and production capabilities that can supply the extensive products required to support MEF-level planning and execution.
- Provide dissemination systems that link widely dispersed and rapidly manoeuvring forces.
- Provide area specialists and linguists with skills that are pertinent to the AO.
- Support force sustainment operations through detailed logistic intelligence.
- Support force protection efforts conducted throughout a large operating area, with emphasis on the security of critical rear area C2 and logistic facilities.

Planning and Direction

Intelligence direction during sustained operations ashore will be centralized during the planning phase and increasingly decentralized during execution. IRs are extensive and cover all aspects of the threat and the battlespace. Comprehensive collection, production, and dissemination efforts will be required to satisfy these requirements. Detailed management is necessary to ensure that these efforts are properly focused and integrated to meet the needs of the entire force. The MAGTF intelligence section will act as the primary intelligence node, developing intelligence to support the MAGTF commander, staff, and subordinate elements. The Marine component headquarters serves as the focal point for connectivity with the theater or JTF intelligence structure. During the planning phase, timeliness of intelligence production may not be as critical because the planning process for sustained operations ashore normally takes place over an extended period and offers the opportunity to use more time and resources to answer those requirements.

Intelligence Cycle	*Key Considerations*
Planning and direction.	MAGTF acting as central mode. Need for broad intelligence structure with extensive liaison requirements.
Collection.	Competition for national, theater, and JTF support. Reliance on organic assets to satisfy many tactical requirements. Support to BDA.
Processing, exploitation, and production.	Wide-scope effort that bridges operational and tactical levels. Importance of target and geographic intelligence.
Dissemination.	Extensive CIS infrastructure. Widely dispersed units. Timely support.
Utilization.	Need to integrate operational and tactical levels of intelligence and operations. Support to sustainability functions.

Figure 6-1. *Intelligence Considerations During Sustained Operations Ashore.*

Once execution begins, the emphasis is on satisfaction of time-sensitive requirements to support operational and tactical decisionmaking. Intelligence nodes will be created at selected times and places to provide tailored intelligence support to units executing specific phases or aspects of the concept of operations. Intelligence direction must balance the support provided among close, deep, and rear operations and the support to current and future operations.

The intelligence structure required to support sustained operations ashore is normally more extensive than that used in other types of MAGTF operations. A detailed planning effort must be undertaken to ensure that the necessary assets are tasked, deployed, and positioned where and when they are required.

Sustained operations ashore are frequently based on a theater combatant commander's approved operations plan or other standing contingency plans that include provisions for a baseline intelligence support structure. These plans must be adapted and tailored to the particulars of the current and projected operational situation. Intelligence plans use a building block approach, phasing in capabilities to keep pace with the buildup of operational forces. Planners must remain aware that intelligence capabilities must be in place to support the earliest steps of the planning phase; therefore, a robust intelligence structure is normally required in the initial stages of the deployment.

Many of the intelligence activities conducted during sustained operations ashore will be joint. Intelligence plans must provide for connectivity with the theater or joint and other component intelligence assets and for participation in theater or JTF intelligence mechanisms. An extensive liaison effort will be required to ensure that MAGTF IRs and operations are fully coordinated with those of joint and other Service intelligence activities. The MARFOR and MAGTF will require significant personnel augmentation to meet the broad scope of intelligence activities in sustained operations ashore and provide liaison teams to the numerous joint and supporting force intelligence agencies. This augmentation can be drawn from residual forces, the supporting establishment or the Reserves.

Collection

Sustained operations ashore will normally be supported by the full range of national- and theaterlevel collection capabilities and by the organic assets of the participating component forces. Collection priorities for national and theater assets will be determined by the JFC. The bulk of these assets will usually be targeted against overall theater/JTF objectives. Marines must participate in the joint collection management and production processes to ensure that MAGTF PIRs receive appropriate support from the theater/JTF level. However, even if MAGTF requirements are given priority, the results of national and theater collection operations cannot be relied on to completely satisfy the number of requirements developed during extended sustained operations ashore or to provide the level of detail needed for tactical planning and execution. For this reason, the MAGTF must depend on its organic collection assets to provide the bulk of its tactical intelligence information, particularly during the execution phase. The MAGTF must be prepared to plan and execute imagery, SIGINT, HUMINT, ground reconnaissance, and CI force protection source operations throughout its AO. This includes collection activities in support of deep operations and the planning of future operations. MAGTF collection plans must be coordinated with those of higher, adjacent, and supporting commands to ensure the following:

- All requirements receive adequate coverage.
- Collection assets are employed efficiently with minimal overlaps.
- Collection operations are sufficiently integrated to permit free exchange of collection targeting data and tracking of collection targets as they move through the battlespace.

Processing, Exploitation, and Production

Processing, exploitation, and production efforts in support of sustained operations ashore parallel those for OMFTS. The scope of the initial production is broad, with the focus narrowing as particular COAs are selected and a concept of operations is developed. Geographic intelligence production takes on added importance. Geographic intelligence helps identify opportunities for ground and air maneuver and determine line-of-sight profiles for observation, weapons employment, and the effective use of communications-electronic equipment. Mapping enhancements, lines-of communications studies, and IPB graphics (such as cross-country mobility, weather effects, and combined obstacle overlays) are key intelligence products that support sustained operations ashore.

Threat analysis must be comprehensive and generally deals with large ground and air formations. This analysis covers reserves and committed forces and must consider all factors that affect the enemy's ability to fight at the operational and tactical levels, including leadership, doctrine, training, readiness, and sustainability. An extensive production effort is devoted to supporting CSS operations.

The main components of this effort are studies on the local climate, infrastructure, and resources and on the threat to our rear area and lines of communications. Products from national, theater, and JTF intelligence agencies contribute to the production effort, but many of these products will have to be tailored by the AFC and GCE, ACE, and CSSE intelligence sections to satisfy particular MAGTF requirements. During execution, emphasis is placed on rapid processing and production of tactical intelligence to support decisionmaking in the current battle, while at the same time providing detailed intelligence to shape plans for future operations.

Dissemination

The ability to develop and maintain a shared picture of the battlespace among the diverse components of the joint force is essential. MAGTF and Marine component dissemination architectures not only must provide for distributing intelligence within the MAGTF, but also must permit the timely exchange of intelligence with the theater or JTF headquarters, other component commands, and adjacent and supporting units. Marine intelligence architectures must be fully integrated with the theater or JTF structures. This requires detailed planning and coordination because each theater and JTF has a unique architecture and sometimes separate channels are used for the dissemination of finished intelligence, imagery, SIGINT, HUMINT, and CI information. Dissemination during the early phases is normally simplified by establishing a reliable, redundant communications system between fixed or semi-fixed CPs. However, even a robust communications system will be challenged by the requirement to distribute a large volume of maps, imagery, and other graphic products during the planning stage.

During execution, the dissemination challenges are similar to those of OMFTS; i.e., ensuring the rapid distribution of time sensitive, mission-critical intelligence to widely dispersed units on the move or in contact with the enemy. A number of techniques can be used to prevent the loss of intelligence that is needed for timely decisionmaking in the stream of intelligence data and information. Some follow:

- Establishing alarm dissemination channels.

- Using broadcast mode for specialized intelligence reporting.
- Employing DSTs or designating a specific element of the intelligence section as a dissemination team.
- Linking dissemination to factors developed in the other phases of intelligence development, such as PIRs, named areas of interest, highvalue targets, and high-payoff targets.
- Giving particular attention to the distribution of updated imagery and graphic intelligence products to units that cannot be supported from fixed or semi-fixed intelligence support nodes.

Utilization

The use of intelligence in sustained operations ashore follows the same principles as its use in OMFTS. The difference lies in the scope of the effort required and the need to integrate intelligence and operations simultaneously at multiple levels: theater or JTF, MARFOR, MAGTF, MSC, and tactical units (regiments/groups/battalions/squadrons/detachments).

In sustained operations ashore, intelligence is used to form operational and tactical plans that will accomplish campaign objectives. Broad-based strategic, operational, and tactical intelligence on the enemy and the AO is used by intelligence and operational planners in an interactive process to identify COG and critical vulnerabilities that can be attacked or exploited to achieve campaign objectives. This in turn leads to COA development, selection, and refinement, an effort that must be coordinated and integrated from the theater/JTF down to the tactical level. Intelligence helps determine the main and supporting efforts; designate objectives, times, and locations for these efforts; and identify the support required for each to succeed. During execution, intelligence helps develop the situation, supporting decisions on whether to continue or modify the plan and whether to exploit success or take advantage of new opportunities. At the same time, intelligence facilitates the planning of follow-on operations through support to combat assessment and providing continuing IPB analysis. Intelligence helps plan and conduct critical sustainability functions, contributing key logistic intelligence and force protection recommendations.

Chapter - 7

Military Operations Other Than War

MOOTW refers to the conduct of Marine and naval expeditionary operations across the range of military operations short of war. MOOTW encompass a wide variety of activities intended to deter war, resolve conflict, promote peace, and support civil authorities. MOOTW encompass a broad range of 16 possible missions and tasks, each of which has its own unique IRs. (See MCDP 1-0.)

Intelligence activities in MOOTW are characterized by the following:

- The initial lack of detailed intelligence databases on the AO.
- An extensive list of nonstandard IRs that must be satisfied to support planning and execution.
- A rapidly changing situation resulting from crisis conditions in the AO.
- A compressed time frame for intelligence development.
- Restrictions on collection operations.

Intelligence shapes operations during MOOTW as it does during other types of expeditionary operations. However, in addition to understanding the physical environment and the threat, the commander must have intelligence on political, economic, and sociological conditions to develop sound military plans that will accomplish the assigned mission.

To support MOOTW, MAGTF intelligence operations and supporting assets must be maintained in a high state of readiness.

MAGTF intelligence sections must focus on areas with the greatest potential for executing contingency operations and must be able to respond with minimal warning and preparation. They must also be flexibile to adapt to the wide variety of potential missions, possessing the expertise and specialized capabilities to provide intelligence across the full range of MOOTW.

Required Intelligence Capabilities

- Forward-deployed intelligence sections that are manned, trained, and equipped to respond to a variety of short-notice contingency operations.
- Deployable intelligence assets that can be rapidly "surged" to augment the capabilities of a forward- deployed MAGTF committed to MOOTW.
- Specialized knowledge concerning infrastructure, political, economic, cultural, and sociological conditions in a variety of geographic areas.
- The ability to perform IPB and situation development that focuses on unconventional threat forces, such as security forces, paramilitary groups, insurgents, and terrorists.
- Organic CI and HUMINT capability that is prepared for operation in a variety of MOOTW scenarios.
- SIGINT assets that can collect information from nontraditional targets.
- Dissemination systems that link widely dispersed forces.
- Connectivity to national, theater, joint, and multinational force intelligence assets to provide intelligence support during planning and execution.
- Area specialists and linguists with skills that are pertinent to the AO.
- Expertise in the operations and functioning of non-DOD government agencies, international coalitions, and nongovernmental organizations (NGOs). (An NGO is a transnational organization of private citizens that maintains a consultative status with the United Nations. NGOs may

be professional associations, foundations, businesses or groups with a common interest in humanitarian assistance. Examples include the Red Cross and the Cooperative for Assistance and Relief Everywhere.)

Planning and Direction

There are certain unique intelligence considerations during MOOTW. (See figure 7-1.) Direction of the intelligence effort in MOOTW will generally be highly decentralized. During MOOTW, MAGTF elements can be spread across a wide area, each with a different mission and facing a unique situation. While a central node will be needed to direct the efforts of MAGTF intelligence assets and coordinate external support, the bulk of intelligence will be provided by subordinate intelligence sections supporting their individual units. Consideration should be given to directing the intelligence effort on an area-support basis rather than a unit support basis. In an area-support system, intelligence nodes are created to support all units operating in the designated area. IRs will be extensive and diverse. Many will deal with topics and threats that are not normally confronted during conventional operations. Individual intelligence sections and nodes must be provided with expertise or with access to resources that can satisfy these nonstandard requirements.

MOOTW are often generated as a result of fast-moving crisis situations. Intelligence plans must emphasize readiness and flexibility to respond to MOOTW requirements in a timely manner. MAGTF intelligence sections at all levels must maintain an awareness of potential contingency missions and adopt a "lean forward" approach toward anticipating requirements. Forward-deployed MAGTFs must possess all required intelligence capabilities to function in a wide variety of MOOTW missions. The active Marine service components (Marine Forces Atlantic or Pacific) must be prepared to rapidly deploy additional or specialized assets to augment the capabilities of the forward-deployed MAGTF.

In planning the intelligence structure required to support a particular MOOTW, several factors must be considered. The

MAGTF intelligence section, whether afloat or ashore, must have connectivity to all supporting external intelligence agencies. It is often necessary to augment subordinate intelligence sections to provide an enhanced capability to support the independent activities of their units. There are normally extensive contacts with organizations outside the US military command structure during MOOTW. Liaison and information exchange with non-DOD agencies and NGOs and multinational and/or host nation military and security forces must be anticipated.

Intelligence Cycle	*Key Considerations*
Planning and direction.	Decentralized direction. Need for muliple intelligence support nodes with specialized capabilities.
Collection.	Nonstandard requirements. Importance of HUMINT, CI, and nontraditional collection activities.
Processing, exploitation, and production. Dissemination.	Focus on infrastructure, political, economic, and sociological factors. Use of nonstandard production formats. Large number of independent units operating throughout the area.
Utilization.	Intelligence exchange with joint, multinational, and nonmilitary units. Need to monitor effectiveness and effect of ongoing operations. Support to force protection, civil affairs, PSYOP, and sustainability.

Figure 7-1. *Intelligence Considerations in MOOTW.*

Collection

Because MOOTW present nontraditional targets, collection operations must blend the capabilities and limitations of all available assets. Satisfaction of unique MOOTW requirements often requires the use of specialized capabilities or innovative approaches to the employment of standard assets.

During the planning and initial phases of the operation, national and theater assets will be relied on to satisfy basic requirements concerning entry points, infrastructure, and conventional aspects of the threat. Because supporting intelligence agencies often have limited capabilities in MOOTW situations, organic assets are brought to bear as early as possible, including being employed as part of the advance party or lead element of the force. The nature of the MOOTW environment, threat, and requirements often present a lucrative opportunity for the conduct of HUMINT and CI collections operations. A MAGTF committed to a MOOTW must have a robust CI and HUMINT capability, augmented by appropriate area specialist and linguist support. This capability should be deployed as soon as practical to initiate force protection collection operations and establish necessary liaisons. The MAGTF must also exploit open sources and maintain contact with non-DOD government agencies and NGOs.

Processing, Exploitation, and Production

Intelligence production requirements in MOOTW are normally focused on nontraditional subject areas. For example, detailed knowledge of the host nation's economic, transportation, medical, and public works infrastructure will be required to develop plans for humanitarian assistance operations. Threat studies to support a peacekeeping mission must encompass an extensive treatment of political, cultural, and sociological factors related to various insurgent or paramilitary factions in addition to the threat's military capabilities. Use of area specialists and expertise from external intelligence organizations, non-DOD agencies (State Department, US Agency for International Development, etc.), and NGOs is crucial to satisfying these requirements. Production formats must be adapted to the requirements of a particular situation. Normal IPB analysis must be modified to highlight factors crucial to the specific

MOOTW mission. Processing and production in MOOTW must be responsive to the needs of the numerous small elements that may be conducting independent activities throughout the AO. Production in support of these elements must be tailored to specific mission requirements and provide details pertinent to the small-unit level. Intelligence that increases the situational awareness of individual Marines, such as information on local customs, language, and health and sanitation, is an important part of this effort.

Dissemination

Dissemination during MOOTW must provide for the timely distribution of intelligence to a large number of elements that are widely dispersed throughout the AO. Creating intelligence support nodes for a specific area or region will aid the dissemination effort, but only if these nodes are equipped to receive all-source intelligence (in particular imagery and graphic products) from supporting collection and production agencies. Dissemination plans must also include provisions for the exchange of intelligence with other Service and multinational units participating in the operation, non-DOD agencies, and NGOs. Interoperability, sanitation, declassification, and releasability must all be considered and determined before such exchanges can occur.

Utilization

Intelligence shapes the planning and execution of MOOTW just as it does in other types of operations. During planning, intelligence helps determine the nature and scope of the operations and tasks required to accomplish the mission, the size and type of forces required, and the location and duration of the effort required. During execution, intelligence is used to enhance the effectiveness of ongoing operations, assess the results of completed activities, and identify follow-on missions and tasks that will help accomplish the overall objective. Emphasis is also placed on intelligence support of specialized functions that have enhanced importance during MOOTW: logistics, force protection, civil affairs, and PSYOP.

Chapter - 8

Joint Operations and Multinational Operations

A coordinated intelligence effort makes a critical contribution to the success of joint operations. MAGTFs participate in full partnership with other Services in joint operations. MAGTF intelligence operations are fully integrated with joint intelligence activities to ensure unity of effort, mutual support, and effective employment of limited intelligence resources.

Multinational operations are "military actions conducted by forces of two or more nations, typically organized within the structure of a coalition or alliance." MARFORs may participate in a wide variety of multinational operations, ranging from routine bilateral exercises to coalition warfare in major regional contingencies. Instances of unilateral US military operations are becoming less frequent, particularly in MOOTW. Marine units must be prepared to carry out intelligence operations in the context of multinational operations.

Effective intelligence support in joint operations depends on the following:

- Agreement on policies and procedures.
- Mutual intelligence support.
- Shared intelligence capabilities and assets.
- Full interoperability and connectivity among participants.
- Robust liaison.

JFC and Component Commander

Responsibilities

JFCs are responsible for all aspects of intelligence support within their commands. They have the responsibility and authority to determine, direct, and coordinate all mission-related collection and analysis activities through centralized or apportioned collection and production management efforts. Component commanders remain responsible for the intelligence function within their commands and use organic intelligence capabilities to support their assigned missions. The JFC makes national, theater, and joint force intelligence assets available to support the efforts of the component commanders. At the same time, component capabilities must be available to assist the joint intelligence effort.

Joint Intelligence Structure

The JFC is assisted in carrying out intelligence responsibilities by the joint force J-2. The J-2 exercises many of the JFC's intelligence functions while acting as the senior intelligence officer in the joint force. Intelligence assets of the joint force headquarters are consolidated in a JISE. The combatant (theater) command is supported by a JIC, which is a standing intelligence element. A JISE is a temporary agency established to provide support to a particular JTF. The JISE provides intelligence support to the JFC and the entire joint force. Marine intelligence specialists will be assigned to the JISE to articulate Marine capabilities and requirements, influence decisions, and optimize intelligence support to the Marine component. Key functions performed by the JISE follow:

- Centralized collection, production, and dissemination management for joint force and supporting intelligence assets.
- All-source intelligence production to satisfy JFC and component requirements.
- Developing and maintaining data bases that support planning, operations, and targeting.
- Producing target studies and materials.

- Providing access to supporting national and theater intelligence assets.

Each theater establishes its own intelligence architecture, providing connectivity between the national- and theater-level intelligence organizations, the JTF, and its component commands. MARFOR and MAGTF intelligence architectures must be able to plug into the architectures of any theater where they might be employed.

Procedures

Joint intelligence activities are governed by joint intelligence doctrine contained in *Joint Doctrine for Intelligence Support to Operations*, and supporting manuals in the 2-series of JPs. Joint intelligence doctrine is supplemented by combatant commanders' TTP for intelligence developed by each theater command. During joint operations, Marine intelligence activities will adhere to joint doctrine and any published theater TTP pertaining to that operation.

Marine Intelligence Section and Unit Responsibilities

- Operate in accordance with joint intelligence doctrine, theater TTP, and individual JTF procedures.
- Participate in joint intelligence mechanisms to coordinate collection management, intelligence production, HUMINT and SIGINT collection operations, target intelligence support, intelligencearchitectures, CI activities and collection operations, and other intelligence operations.
- Provide intelligence support to the joint force headquarters or other JTF components as directed.
- Contribute personnel and other assets to augment the J-2 section and JISE if requested.
- Employ joint or other component intelligence assets.
- Enter the JTF intelligence architecture.
- Exchange liaison elements with the J-2, JISE, and/or other JTF components as required.

MARFOR Component Headquarters or MAGTF CE as a JTF Headquarters

A Marine component headquarters or a MAGTF CE may be designated to provide the nucleus of a JTF headquarters. The MARFOR or MAGTF G-2 must be prepared to function as the JTF J-2, with the G-2's intelligence section serving as the base for establishing a JISE. To carry out this function, MARFOR and MEF G-2 sections must prepare plans for operating as a JTF J-2 and conduct the training to be able to execute these plans. Plans should be based on joint doctrine and theater TTP and should include J-2/JISE organization, personnel and equipment requirements (with their augmentation sources), a baseline intelligence architecture, and standing operating procedures. Each MARFOR and MEF G-2 section should establish a standing JTF intelligence planning cell made up of intelligence specialists who are knowledgeable in joint force and other Service intelligence capabilities, limitations, and operating procedures to develop these plans.

Multinational Operations

There is no single intelligence doctrine for multinational operations. Each coalition or alliance must develop its own doctrine. The coalition commander determines standardized procedures for coalition forces. NATO standardization agreements (STANAGs) and quadripartite standing agreements among US, British, Canadian, and Australian forces provide standards and guidance to conduct military operations by forces in these alliances. STANAG 2936, *Intelligence Doctrine*, governs intelligence operations. Joint intelligence doctrine and architectures provide a framework for developing the multinational intelligence support structure. Multinational intelligence operations are based on the following principles:

- Maintain unity of effort. Intelligence operations must be directed at the common threat. A threat to one alliance member should be considered a threat to all.

Make adjustments: Effective multinational operations require minimizing the differences in national concepts of intelligence support. Commanders and their intelligence officers must be willing to make adjustments to national procedures to share intelligence and integrate intelligence operations. Special arrangements should be considered for developing, communicating, and using intelligence where there are differences in nations' language, culture, doctrine, terminology, organization, and equipment.

Plan early and concurrently: Multinational forces' IRs and procedures should be identified, planned, coordinated, and exercised before execution.

Share all necessary intelligence: Each coalition member should share intelligence that supports planning and execution. However, information about intelligence sources and methods should not be shared unless absolutely necessary. The methodology for exchanging intelligence should be developed and exercised before operations begin. Authorization for foreign disclosure should be obtained and procedures for sanitation and declassification should be developed as part of this planning process. During execution, the exchange must be monitored and adapted to ensure that it is meeting the needs of all coalition partners.

Conduct complementary intelligence operations: Each nation's intelligence assets capitalize on their strengths and offset the weaknesses of other members' assets, providing the coalition with the most effective blend of capabilities.

Many potential allies may not possess the range of US intelligence capabilities; therefore, US intelligence sections must expect to take the lead in developing intelligence during multinational operations. Particular attention must be given to provisions for sanitation, declassification, and releasability of intelligence developed by US forces and agencies to coalition partners. Personnel who are knowledgeable in these techniques and procedures must be included in the MAGTF or Marine component intelligence section. Intelligence plans must provide for connectivity with multinational forces and liaison elements with appropriate linguistic and area specialist skills.

Appendix
Glossary

Section I. Acronyms

ACE	aviation combat element
AC/S	assistant chief of staff
AFC	all-source fusion center
AFP	all-source fusion platoon
AIntP	Allied Intelligence Publication
AO	area of operations
ATARS	advanced tactical airborne reconnaissance system
ATFIC	amphibious task force intelligence center
BDA	battle damage assessment
C2	command and control
C2W	command and control warfare
CCIR	commander's critical information requirements
CE	command element
CGS	common ground station
CHATS	CI/HUMINT automated tool set
CI	counterintelligence
CIA	Central Intelligence Agency
CIC	combat intelligence center
CIS	communications and information systems

CMDO	collection management/dissemination officer
Co	company
COA	course of action
COG	center of gravity
COP	common operational picture
CP	command post
CSS	combat service support
CSSE	combat service support element
CTP	common tactical picture
CV	critical vulnerability
DIA	Defence Intelligence Agency
DMS	Defence Message System
DOD	Department of Defence
DST	direct support team
EW	electronic warfare
FBI	Federal Bureau of Investigation
FRAGO	fragmentary order
FSCC	fire support coordination center
FSSG	force service support group
GCE	ground combat element
GI&S	geospatial information and services
GSP	ground sensor platoon
HET	HUMINT exploitation team
HLZ	helicopter landing zone
HUMINT	human intelligence
I&W	indications and warning
IAS	intelligence analysis system
ICR	intelligence collection requirement

IDR	intelligence dissemination requirement
IIP	imagery intelligence platoon
IMA	individual mobilization augmentee
IMINT	imagery intelligence
intel bn	intelligence battalion
IO	information operations
IOC	intelligence operations center
IOS	intelligence operations server
IOW	intelligence operations workstation
IPB	intelligence preparation of the battlespace
IPR	intelligence production requirement
IR	intelligence requirement
ISC	intelligence support coordinator
JIC	joint intelligence center
JISE	joint intelligence support element
JSTARS	Joint Surveillance Target Attack Radar System
JTF	joint task force
JWICS	Joint Worldwide Intelligence Communication System
MAGTF	Marine air-ground task force
MARFOR	Marine Corps forces
MARFORRES	Marine Forces Reserve
MASINT	measurement and signature intelligence
MAW	Marine aircraft wing
MCDP.	Marine Corps doctrinal publication
MCIA	Marine Corps Intelligence Activity
MCWP	Marine Corps warfighting publication

MEB	Marine Expeditionary Brigade
MEF	Marine Expeditionary Force
MEU	Marine Expeditionary Unit
MEU(SOC)	Marine Expeditionary Unit (Special Operations Capable)
MIDB	modernized integrated database
MOOTW	military operations other than war
MSC	major subordinate command
NGO	nongovernmental organization
NIMA	National Imagery and Mapping Agency
NMITC	Navy-Marine Corps Intelligence Training Center
NIPRNET	Nonsecure Internet Protocol Router Network
NIST	National Intelligence Support Team NSA National Security Agency
OCAC	operations control and analysis center
OIC	officer in charge
OMFTS	operational manoeuvre from the sea
OODA	observe, orient, decide, and act
OP	observation post
OPCON	operational control
OPLAN	operation plan
OPORD	operational order
OPSEC	operations security
OSINT	open-source intelligence
P&A	production and analysis
PDE&A	planning, decision, execution, and assessment
PIR	priority intelligence requirements
PSYOP	psychological operations

R&S	reconnaissance and surveillance
recon	reconnaissance
rep	representative
RRS	remote receiver station
SARC	surveillance and reconnaissance cell
SIDS	secondary imagery dissemination system
SIGINT	signals intelligence
SIPRNET	Secret Internet Protocol Router Network
SSU	SIGINT support unit
STANAG	standardization agreement
TCAC	Technical Control and Analysis Center
TDN	tactical data network
TEG	Technical Exploitation Group
TERPES	tactical electronic reconnaissance processing and evaluation system
TGTINTEL	target intelligence
TRAP	tactical recovery of aircraft and personnel
TPC	topographic production capability
TRSS	tactical remote sensor system
TTP	tactics, techniques, and procedures
UAV	unmanned aerial vehicle
VMU	Marine unmanned aerial vehicle squadron Section

II. Definitions

all-source intelligence—Intelligence products and/or organizations and activities that incorporate all sources of information, including, most frequently, human resources intelligence, imagery intelligence, measurement and signature intelligence, signals intelligence, and open source data, in the production of finished intelligence.

battle damage assessment—1. The timely and accurate estimate of damage resulting from the application of military force, either lethal or nonlethal, against a predetermined objective. Battle damage assessment can be applied to the employment of all types of weapon systems (air, ground, naval, and special forces weapon systems) throughout the range of military operations. Battle damage assessment is primarily an intelligence responsibility with required inputs and coordination from the operators. Battle damage assessment is composed of physical damage assessment, unctional damage assessment, and target system assessment. Also called BDA. **2.** The timely and accurate estimate of the damage resulting from the application of military force. BDA estimates physical damage to a particular target, functional damage to that target, and the capability of the entire target system to continue its operations.

centers of gravity—1. Those characteristics, capabilities, or localities from which a military force derives its freedom of action, physical strength, or will to fight. Also called COG. **2.** A key source of strength without which an enemy cannot function.

collection—The gathering of intelligence data and information to satisfy the identified requirements.

collection management—1. The process of converting intelligence requirements into collection requirements, establishing priorities, and tasking or coordinating with appropriate collection sources or agencies, monitoring results and retasking, as required. **2.** Its purpose is to conduct an effective effort to collect all necessary data while ensuring the efficient use of limited and valuable collection assets.

combat data—Data derived from reporting by operational units.

command and control—1. The exercise of authority and direction by a properly designated commander over assigned and attached forces in the accomplishment of the mission. Command and control functions are performed through an arrangement of personnel, equipment, communications, facilities, and procedures employed by a commander in planning, directing, coordinating, and controlling forces and operations in the accomplishment of the mission. Also called C2. **2.** The means by which a commander recognizes what needs to be done and sees to it that appropriate actions are taken. Commander's critical information requirements—

Information regarding the enemy and friendly activities and the environment identified by the commander as critical to maintaining situational awareness, planning future activities, and facilitating timely decisionmaking. Also called CCIR.

commander's intent—A commander's clear, concise personal articulation of the reason(s) behind one or more tasks assigned to a subordinate. It is one of two components of every mission statement which supports the higher and/ or supported commander's intent and guides the exercise of initiative in the absence of instructions.

counterintelligence—Within the Marine Corps, CI constitutes active and passive measures intended to deny a threat force valuable information about the friendly situation, to detect and neutralize hostile intelligence collection, and to deceive the enemy as to friendly capabilities and intentions. Also called CI.

critical vulnerability—An aspect of a center of gravity that if exploited will do the most significant damage to an adversary's ability to resist. Also called CV.

descriptive intelligence—Class of intelligence which describes existing and previously existing conditions intended to promote situational awareness. Descriptive intelligence has two components: basic intelligence, which is general background knowledge about established and relatively constant conditions; and current intelligence, which is concerned with describing the existing situation.

dissemination—Conveyance of intelligence to users in a suitable form.

dissemination management—Involves establishing dissemination priorities, selecting dissemination means, and monitoring the flow of intelligence throughout the command. The objective of dissemination management is to deliver the required intelligence to the appropriate user in proper form at the right time while ensuring that individual consumers and the dissemination system are not overloaded by attempting to move unneeded or irrelevant information. Dissemination management also provides for use of security controls that do not impede the timely delivery or subsequent use of intelligence while protecting intelligence sources and methods.

estimative intelligence—Class of intelligence which attempts to anticipate future possibilities and probabilities based upon descriptive intelligence in the context of planned enemy and friendly operations.

human intelligence—1. A category of intelligence derived from information collected and provided by human sources. **2.** HUMINT operations cover a wide range of activities encompassing

reconnaissance patrols, aircrew reports and debriefs, debriefing of refugees, interrogations of prisoners of war, and the conduct of CI force protection source operations. Also called HUMINT.

imagery intelligence—Intelligence derived from the exploitation of collection by visual photography, infrared sensors, lasers, electrooptics, and radar sensors such as synthetic aperture radar wherein images of objects are reproduced optically or electronically on film, electronic display devices, or other media. Also called IMINT.

indications and warning—Those intelligence activities intended to detect and report time-sensitive intelligence information on foreign developments that could involve a threat to the United States or allied military, political, or economic interests or to US citizens abroad. It includes forewarning of enemy actions or intentions; the imminence of hostilities; insurgency; nuclear/non-nuclear attack on the United States, its overseas forces, or allied nations; hostile reactions to United States reconnaissance activities; terrorists' attacks; and other similar events. Also called I&W.

intelligence—1. The product resulting from the collection, processing, integration, analysis, evaluation, and interpretation of available information concerning foreign countries or areas. **2.** Information and knowledge about an adversary obtained through observation, investigation, analysis, or understanding. **3.** Knowledge of the enemy and the surrounding environment that is needed to support decisionmaking.

intelligence cycle—The steps by which informationis converted into intelligence and made available to users.

intelligence data—Data derived from assets primarily dedicated to intelligence collection: imagery systems, electronic intercept equipment, human intelligence sources, and so on.

intelligence discipline—A well-defined area of intelligence collection, processing, exploitation, and reporting using a specific category of technical or human resources. There are five major disciplines: human intelligence, imagery intelligence, measurement and signature intelligence, signals intelligence (communications intelligence, electronic intelligence, and foreign instrumentation signals intelligence), and open-source intelligence.

intelligence operations—The variety of intelligence tasks that are carried out by various intelligence organizations and activities. Intelligence preparation of the battlespace—

1. An analytical methodology employed to reduce uncertainties concerning the enemy, environment, and terrain for all types of operations. Intelligence preparation of the battlespace builds an extensive data base for each potential area in which a unit may be required to operate. The data base is then analyzed in detail to determine the impact of the enemy, environment, and terrain on operations and presents it in graphic form. Intelligence preparation of the battlespace is a continuing process. Also called IPB. **2.** A systematic, continuous process of analyzing the threat and environment in a specific geographic area.

intelligence requirement—**1.** Any subject, general or specific, upon which there is a need for the collection of information, or the production of intelligence. Also called IR. **2.** Questions about the enemy and the environment, the answers to which a commander requires to make sound decisions.

joint force—A general term applied to a force composed of significant elements, assigned or attached, of two or more Military Departments, operating under a single joint force commander.

joint intelligence center—The intelligence center of the joint force headquarters. The joint intelligence center is responsible for providing and producing the intelligence required to support the joint force commander and staff, components, task forçes and elements, and the national intelligence community. Also called JIC.

joint operations—A general term to describe military actions conducted by joint forces, or by Service forces in relationships (e.g., support, coordinating authority), which, of themselves, do not create joint forces.

main effort—The designated subordinate unit whose mission at a given point in time is most critical to the overall mission success.

maneuver warfare—A warfighting philosophy that seeks to shatter the enemy's cohesion through a variety of rapid, focused, and unexpected actions which create a turbulent and rapidly deteriorating situation with which the enemy cannot cope. Measurement and signature intelligence—

1. Scientific and technical intelligence obtained by quantitative and qualitative analysis of data (metric, angle, spatial, wavelength, time dependence, modulation, plasma, and hydromagnetic) derived from specific technical sensors for the purpose of identifying any distinctive features associated with the target. The detected feature may be either reflected or emitted. Also called MASINT.

2. Intelligence information gathered by technical instruments such as radars, passive electrooptical sensors, radiation detectors, and remote ground sensors.

open-source intelligence—

1. Information of potential intelligence value that is available to the general public. Also called OSINT.

2. OSINT sources include books, magazines, newspapers, maps, commercial electronic networks and databases, and radio and television broadcasts. OSINT involves no information that is classified at its origin or acquired through controlled collection.

priority intelligence requirements—

1. Those intelligence requirements for which a commander has an anticipated and stated priority in his task of planning and decisionmaking. Also called PIR. **2.** An intelligence requirement MCWP 2-1 Intelligence Operations A-5 associated with a decision that will critically affect the overall success of the command's mission.

production management—Encompasses determining the scope, content, and format of each product; developing a plan and schedule for the development of each product; assigning priorities among the various IPRs; allocating processing, exploitation, and production resources; and integrating production efforts with collection and dissemination.

sensor data—Data derived from sensors whose primary mission is surveillance or target acquisition: air surveillance radars, counterbattery radars, and remote ground sensors.

signals intelligence—

1. A category of intelligence comprising either individually or in combination all communications intelligence, electronics intelligence, and foreign instrumentation signals intelligence, however transmitted.

2. Intelligence derived from communications, electronics, and foreign instrumentation signals. Also called SIGINT.

situational awareness—Knowledge and understanding of the current situation which provides timely, relevant and accurate assessment of friendly, enemy and other operations within the battlespace. Also called SA.

tactical intelligence—

1. Intelligence that is required for planning and conducting tactical operations. **2.** Tactical intelligence concerns itself primarily with the location, capabilities, and possible intentions of enemy units on the battlefield and with the tactical aspects of terrain and weather.

warfighting functions—The six mutually supporting military activities integrated in the conduct of all military operations: command and control, intelligence, manoeuvre, fires, logistics, and force protection.

INDEX